Bridal Shower Handbook

The Complete Guide to Planning the Perfect Party

GAIL GRECO

Cover design and interior layout: Anthony Jacobson
Editor: Stephen Levy

Cover photograph by Perry L. Struse, Jr.
Illustrations by Harry Blair

Library of Congress Catalog Card Number 87-51440

ISBN 0-87069-510-X

10 9 8 7 6 5 4 3 2

Published by

Wallace-Homestead

A Capital Cities/ABC, Inc. Company

Wallace-Homestead Book Company
201 King of Prussia Road
Radnor, Pennsylvania 19089

For my husband, Tom Bagley, who showers me daily with gifts of time, patience, editorial assistance, and his endearing sense of humor. He is my tireless cheerleader.

Contents

Preface

It was 1976 when I gave my first theme bridal shower. I wanted to prepare a memorable party for a special relative. Running to the store for a bunch of typical premade decorations or turning the party over to a caterer or restaurant seemed like the easy way out—a trite way to honor her. Having given other showers, I was tired of the typical shower entrapments and fanfare that didn't really have any meaning. In short, I was bored with the typical bridal shower. I decided to give her a theme party—an affair of the heart, so to speak. She deserved my time and trouble. I wanted everyone to know how much she was loved. I'm sure you feel the same about your bride.

I was always throwing parties. And even for the smaller ones with only a foursome for a special luncheon or dinner, my get-togethers typically had some sort of theme carried through with decorations, invitations, and food. My goal was to give my guests a dining experience, not just dinner. The parties always met with unsolicited applause. I decided to apply the same planning techniques to the shower. Some of the results of those years of brainstorming and entertaining are included in this book.

I felt it was time to give those facing the responsibility of a bridal shower new alternatives. I have tried to present not just, say, a gardening shower where garden tools and accessories are the gifts for a bride who has no interest in gardening, but a shower for a bride who likes gardening. And not just a sewing shower where everyone gives sewing gifts to a bride who hardly lifts a needle, but a shower for a bride who likes to sew.

These new theme showers will spark lively conversation and provide interesting experiences for your guests. The party will be a hit. But let me caution you that the mark of a good party is not just in its uniqueness or its decorations and food. At the center of all successful parties is the cheerful and relaxed hostess. Prewedding days are harried, and the one giving the shower is often in the midst of that hustle and bustle. So how do you remain calm and pleasant?

I have always believed that good organization produces great results. That theory has never disappointed me. Good organization is the key to achieving an excellent party. As you read through this book, you will find step-by-step information designed to make your shower flow smoothly. Most of the suggestions, even many of the recipes, can be prepared well in advance of the party.

My intent is that you find this book intriguing, thought-provoking, and invaluable for all of your shower needs.

Welcome to the party!

Acknowledgments

Twenty years ago, a newspaper editor with a crusty exterior but a heart made of sugar, gave me the chance of a lifetime. He taught me how to climb the often knotty, tough-skinned ropes of writing and reporting. Furthermore, he believed I could do it and didn't give up on me until I did. Now, it's my turn, Howard Ball, wherever you are, to thank you for putting me on the road of journalism. It has given me a wonderful life.

I would also like to thank my parents, Ann and Bob Greco, for everything, plus the scissors-holder favor. Dot Greco-Brown, my sister, for the sewing shower invitation and other creative ideas. Joanne and Lester Anderson for their longtime friendship and tools for my independent writing career. Diane Sheehan, Marie Vovakes, Diane Stacconi, Michael Larson, Nancy Fanelli, and Linda Rose for their part in preparing this book. Pat Barnes-Svarney for her unrelenting right ear.

Introduction

So you're planning to give a bridal shower, and you want to make it special. Now you can. Whether you're a pro at giving showers or this is your first time, this handbook will help you, the hostess, create a memorable party. Your bride and her guests will walk away exhilarated, having experienced a refreshingly new type of bridal shower, a personal theme shower.

I'm not talking about the typical lingerie, kitchen, or linen shower. Today's bride already has an undergarment wardrobe, cookware, and other hope-chest contents. Nor do I mean the traditional shower with its paper umbrellas and watering-can entrapments. I'm talking about creative party alternatives.

Throwing together sandwich platters, a beverage, and calling it a shower is not good enough for your bride-to-be. You want to put your heart and hands into this event. But how? You will find the answers in this, the most complete book on the subject of bridal showers.

You'll be able to give an affair that directly dedicates itself to your bride and reflects her lifestyle. A shower that is tingling with freshness . . . a party that blends the conventional with the contemporary . . . a gift-giving reception to honor the bride with the time of her life.

Incorporating a specialty theme into the plans will help you achieve this new type of shower. Explored in detail on the following pages, the specialty shower is a thoroughly individualized party, designed according to the bride's interests and background. For example, if she is a dancer, decorations, food, and invitations will revolve around dancing. The gifts and how the hostesses dress may also allude to this toe-tapping art.

Specialty theme showers reflect the bride's occupation, her passions, hobbies, or interest in sports. A shower with a personalized motif can be applied to the bride who is marrying later in life and may already have set up housekeeping as well as it can be applied to the first-time bride.

Developing a shower with a unique focus calls for exercising your imagination and creativity. If you think these qualities are in short supply for you, this book will stimulate your inventive juices and guide you through the fundamental process of conceiving the theme shower. If you already possess these attributes, the suggestions presented here will further nourish and spark your inherent resourcefulness.

There are hundreds of ideas to explore here. Each theme suggests decorations, party favors, invitations, hostess apparel, food, and gift ideas. You may be able to use some of them as they are described. For others, you can substitute your own ideas to suit the theme. For example, if your bride is an accountant, the office party shower would apply for the most part. Instead of a cake made to resemble a typewriter, you may have it designed as a calculator. The Italian and Jewish showers are only two examples of ethnic parties. You would follow the same concepts found in these showers, merely substituting the cultural heritage and regional cooking representative of your bride.

Following the themes, there are lifestyle showers for the second-time bride, the bride and groom together, and a shower for the groom. A specialty theme can be applied.

It's impossible to describe all potential themes since each bride is a unique individual; however, the range of shower subjects presented here will provide you with the knowledge and impetus to design your own one-of-a-kind shower. By understanding how a shower with a topic is prepared, you'll be able to easily add your own ideas—and have fun doing so.

The themes are the main part of this handbook. You'll also find detailed, step-by-step information for planning the shower and important tips for all showers, including modern-day etiquette. There is a Bridal Trivia Game that will entertain as well as acquaint your guests with what inspired the wedding customs we follow today.

Some themes have a full menu suggestion plus recipes. Other themes, because of their nature, have only suggested food ideas. For example, the sewing shower prescribes serving only a snack and beverage, as your company will be working on a sewing machine and there will not be time for a full-course meal. The groom's shower also offers no bill of fare. It advises, instead, that the men order restaurant take-out food.

There is also a bonus section on giving exciting baby showers.

These new theme showers will spark lively conversation and will provide interesting experiences for you and your guests. The party will be a hit.

Using This Book

This handbook provides step-by-step information for creating a personal and exciting shower for your bride-to-be.

Reading all of the themes that follow will entertain you as well as show you the thought process involved in planning a unique bridal shower.

When you are ready to begin planning your event, this is how you do it:

1. Pick the theme from the book that is most appropriate for your bride-to-be. Chapter 1, "Planning the Shower," will help you make this decision. Themes contain ideas for decorations, favors, hostess apparel, invitations, gifts, and the menu. Entertainment is suggested in many themes, where appropriate.

2. Consider variations to the theme that may be necessary or that could enhance your shower. You may only need to identify one of the themes in this handbook as a model for a brand-new theme that you create to suit your bride.

3. Fill out the theme work sheet. This form can be used to keep track of any variations you make in the theme you choose from this book. Or, the form can be your guide for designing the brand new theme that you are tailoring specifically to your bride.

4. Use the handy Guest List form to keep track of invitations and responses. Also record any gift suggestions you may have offered to a guest searching for a gift possibility, so that you do not offer the same gift idea to two guests. When a guest calls in with her r.s.v.p., she may mention what gift she intends to bring to the bride. If she does tell you, record it on the Guest List form. Keeping track of the gift ideas that are circulating among the guests will help prevent any duplication of gifts.

5. Remember to increase or decrease the quantity of each recipe ingredient, according to the number of guests. Select a beverage of your choice unless it is provided in the menu. Most of the themes do not suggest a dessert. The after-meal sweet, unless otherwise specified, is a decorated cake from your bakery. Ask for the cake to be iced in the colors you have selected for decorations.

6. Be sure to read "Tips for All Showers" for any theme you select.
7. Some of the favors include rice. Be sure to check with the church or synagogue before filling these favors. Some houses of worship strictly forbid the throwing of rice and even birdseed after the ceremony. If this is the case, fill the favors with candy-coated almonds for the guests to eat instead.
8. If stores in your area do not carry some of the suggested items for decorations and invitations, ask related stores and see if these items can be ordered through their suppliers. A bridal consultant may also be able to help.
9. Check out the chapter on "Hints for Making Any Party a Success."
10. Read the "Shower Checklist" and follow the suggested time schedule. You are now on your way to a successful party.

Planning
the
Bridal Shower

Chapter 1

Planning
the
Bridal Shower

A few weeks before the wedding, the bride is given an informal party to provide her with gifts in honor of her upcoming wedding and new life. At most showers, only women are invited, and they usually are close friends and relatives of the bride.

The shower also is a reaffirmation of old friends and a reaching out to new friends and family. The bride is showered with lots of gifts. Let's take a look at the origins of the bridal shower to better understand what this tradition is all about.

Origins of the Bridal Shower

Why is this party called a shower and why is the umbrella a symbol of the bridal shower?

The first bridal shower probably occurred in Holland. Folklore suggests that a poor Dutch boy was as generous and philanthropic as he was indigent. He gave all he had to needier individuals. One day he made a marriage proposal, with only love to offer his bride as he had no material possessions. His intended's father was not impressed by the young lad's amorous offer, because, as far as he was concerned, there was nothing in it for his daughter.

The bride's father refused to deliver a dowry to the penniless young man. Neighbors and friends, having previously benefited from the Dutch boy's endowments, returned the favor. They showered his bride with gifts to set up the couple's home. Hence, the first unofficial bridal shower took place.

In America, the shower was originally in the form of a quilting bee. Someone would gather friends and relatives of the bride together to start quilting the engaged woman a cover for her bed. Invited guests also included the bride. Everyone would sit around a large table and work on the quilt together.

Later, this prewedding party became known as a shower, as guests began to give more than the quilt. They literally showered the bride with small, inexpensive gifts. Friends would hang an umbrella from the ceiling and fill it with gifts. The bride would then turn the umbrella over as a cache of gifts tumbled out of the parasol.

Bridal showers are still symbolized by an umbrella, but those little gifts are now small items for the bride's wishing well. The main gifts brought to a shower today are much more expensive than gifts bestowed years ago.

Once upon a time, showers were only held in someone's home. Today, they also take place in restaurants and catering halls. Showers outside the home developed partly because travel became easier, thus distant relatives and friends could make the event. As a result, more space was needed, so hostesses began booking rooms at restaurants to hold all of their guests.

The ideal shower, however, is a small, intimate affair of no more than 25 to 30 guests in the home. A smaller shower gives the bride the chance to spend time with all her guests and to enjoy their company.

When you meet with the other hostesses to plan your shower, carefully consider everyone's proposals and follow the rules of etiquette so that no one can question or criticize the event.

The following guidelines will aid you in planning the perfect shower. Refer to them when carrying out any of the themes in this book or any theme shower you design.

Who Gives a Bridal Shower?

The shower is usually entrusted to the bridal party. But a friend of the bride may also give one. In addition, people who may not be invited to the wedding, such as a group from the bride's place of employment, may prepare a shower.

Etiquette guidelines state that it is not proper for the mother of the bride, nor for the bride's relatives, to give the shower. This guideline can probably be traced back to the first shower, which was presented by friends and neighbors. Today, we have broken tradition. Showers held at catering halls with many guests are costly, and it is not unusual to find the mother of the bride offering to help pay the expenses. Also, a relative of the bride may insist on giving the bride a shower.

If the bridal party is hosting the affair, all of the bridesmaids are the hostesses, but the main responsibility is on the maid who has offered her home as the shower's location. In the case of a restaurant shower, the responsibility is on the attendant in charge of coordinating the event.

If you want to host a shower but are not a member of the bridal party, you may need help in setting up the shower. Ask your own friends for assistance, but remember that you (not your friends) are responsible to cover the cost of expenses.

Who Does What?

Organizing a shower is like arranging a small, informal wedding. And as with any wedding, you'll need some helping hands to make the shower flow smoothly. First decide on the day and time, the theme of the shower, and the location.

Next, decide who will do what. Divide the work into four areas: decorations, invitations, food, and entertainment.

The person in charge of food has to do the shopping and cooking; she should formulate the menu with the other hostesses.

Everyone will work on decorations. Someone must be delegated to shop for supplies, and together the group must work them into the theme of the shower.

Someone with good handwriting and an artistic flair should be in charge of inscribing the invitations. Also, she will buy the postage stamps and mail the calling cards. She may or may not be responsible for the r.s.v.p.'s. That duty should go to the main hostess (usually the one holding the shower in her home). If the shower is scheduled at a public place, then guest responses should be called in to the maid of honor. If invitations are to be handcrafted, then the entire group should work on the project.

The main focus of the shower is opening the gifts. This activity may be all the entertainment planned by the hostesses. During the shower meeting, delegate someone to be in charge of gift tags that accompany each present. As the bride reads the tag or card, she will hand it to this person, who will make sure the card stays with the gift. Tags have been lost at showers and it is embarrassing to the bride if she cannot remember who gave her a particular item. It's up to the bride to record her gifts after the shower and send out thank-you notes. Although the bride thanks her guests individually as she opens each gift during the shower, it is in good taste to follow the verbal appreciation with a personal note.

If you choose to have guests bring their favorite recipe for the bride's kitchen, or a helpful household hint, the entertainment hostess should receive them and later read the ideas to the guests. (See the section "Tips for All Showers" for more information on recipe and household hint cards.)

Everyone collectively works on games, music, or the other forms of entertainment.

Where Should the Shower Be Held?

The guest list and budget will determine where to hold the shower. If there are too many people for a house shower, you'll have to consider a catering hall or restaurant banquet room. The shower will probably cost less if you hold the party in someone's home. The smaller the number of guests, the more intimate you can expect the shower to be.

However, if you must hold it in a public place, you can still provide that homey feeling by introducing a theme. The shower with a special theme is an especially good way to personalize the affair if it is being held at a restaurant or catering hall. A special shower, aimed at the bride's lifestyle, puts you in the role of maître d' and warms the impersonal edge of showering the bride in public.

How Much Will the Shower Cost?

If the bridal party is giving the shower, a budget must be worked up together. One approach is to calculate how much each member can afford to contribute. Stay within that total figure by planning decorations, number of guests and where to hold the shower according to the budget. If money is a factor, limit the number of guests and hold the shower at home. If money is not an important consideration, then proceed with the plans, keeping receipts and bills. Add up the final costs and divide this amount among the bridesmaids after the shower.

Whom Should You Invite?

Bridal showers are intimate occasions, and this should be kept in mind when developing the guest list. Assuming the bridesmaids are giving the shower, they may invite every female member on the wedding guest list, or they may invite only close friends and relatives.

The bridesmaids usually select close friends and relatives from a wedding guest list. If the shower is intended to be a surprise, they should ask the mother of the bride for a wedding reception guest list. Otherwise, they may ask the bride for it. Not every female on the roster has to be invited to the shower. Traditionally, the women are the only ones invited to a bridal shower, but times have changed. Now men are sometimes included.

A shower also may be given by those not asked to the wedding. For example, a friend of the bride's mother may want to hold a small gift-giving reception at her house, even though she is not invited to the wedding.

Three final points regarding invitation protocol:

• It is not your responsibility to serve food or provide a place to stay for out-of-town spouses or friends who have driven your guests to the shower.
• A bride may have more than one shower, but no one should be requested to attend more than one.
• Do not invite someone to the shower if she is not on the wedding guest list.

SHOWER GUEST LIST

GUEST	ADDRESS	REPLY	GIFT SUGGESTIONS

When To Shower the Bride?

A shower unofficially starts the exciting nuptial countdown. It is the first of a series of prewedding parties (unless the bride has been given an engagement party), and it usually occurs four·to six weeks prior to the big day. It may take place at any hour and may be anything from a brunch to a buffet luncheon to a sit-down meal.

Surprise! Surprise?

Another decision is whether to surprise the bride or to tell her a shower is coming her way. This choice is up to the hostesses.

Before making a decision, consider that every bride assumes she will receive a shower. If someone doesn't slip and accidentally mention it to the bride, she may deduce something is up when the ruse to take her to a specific location occurs. For example, a few weeks before the wedding, the hostesses will ask the bride to accompany them shopping or to lunch, when they are really taking her to the shower. The bride begins to suspect something because the hostesses appear to be very anxious. The bride will put various little events and comments together and may suspect it is really a shower.

Some brides will admit they were not surprised, but usually (in order to spare the feelings of the hostesses and the guests) they'll pretend the distractions diverted them from the truth. Think about whether it is really worth all the hard work to try and keep the shower a secret. It may be better to formally invite the bride and to concentrate your energies on planning a special affair rather than on worrying about whether anyone is going to accidentally reveal the plan to the bride.

One way to invite the bride to her shower is to take her out to lunch and announce that a shower is coming her way. Tell her the specific time and date. Do not reveal the details or the theme of the shower. Arrange for someone to chauffeur the bride to the shower. Have the guests arrive 30 minutes before the bride, so she can make a grand entrance. When she walks through the door and sees the theme shower you staged, her face will reflect her surprise, and you can be certain it will be genuine.

Shower
Checklist

Chapter 2

Shower Checklist

Eight to ten weeks before the wedding.
- The Maid of Honor or hostess obtains a copy of the wedding guest list from the bride's family and calls a meeting with the bridesmaids or other hostesses to plan the shower.
- A date for the shower is set. Be sure to notify the groom if the shower is intended to be a surprise. He will probably know if the bride has a commitment for the proposed shower date. Also, if the groom knows the date, he will not make any plans with her for that day. If you don't tell him, you run the risk of the bride arranging a date or meeting that she cannot cancel.
- The hostesses decide where to hold the shower. If a catering hall or restaurant is chosen, the room must be reserved immediately to ensure it will be available.
- The hostesses decide who will be responsible for invitations, shopping for supplies, cooking, and other activities.
- A budget is established.
- The hostesses plan and develop a theme for the shower.
- The invitations are discussed
  1. A guest list is prepared.
  2. The invitation is written.
  3. A decision is made as to who will receive the response phone calls and who will purchase and address the invitations and buy the postage stamps.

- Decorations are planned.
  1. A decision is made as to the type of decorations that will be used, whether to buy, rent, or make them, and where they will be used.
  2. Someone is asked to shop for the supplies.
  3. A meeting date is scheduled (to take place about two weeks later) to work on the party decorations.
  4. The use of party favors is considered and a decision is made.

- Entertainment questions
  1. Will the Bridal Trivia Game (see Chapter 21) or some other game be played?
  2. What type of music, if any, will be played in the background?
  3. Will gift ideas be suggested to correlate with the theme, and will there be a wishing well?

Four to six weeks before the shower.
- Record the list of those invited and the gifts they plan to bring, or the gift suggestions you have offered. Use the Guest List form found in Chapter 1.
  1. Mail the invitations and be certain that a return reply date (r.s.v.p.) is specified for two weeks before the shower.
- Meet with all of the hostesses. Have everyone report what has been accomplished and what remains to be done.
- Decide on a shower-day schedule. Will you eat first and then open gifts? Or will you serve hors d'oeuvres and open gifts before the main course? If you are playing a game, when will it begin—before or after the opening of the gifts?

Two to four weeks before the shower.
- Hold a final meeting of the hostesses.
- Review the shower plan. Obtain a total of the invitation returns.
- Calculate how much food will be required.
- Finish the decorations.
- Order a corsage for the bride and flowers for the table.
- Decide who will look after gift tags as the bride opens her presents.

One week before the shower.
- Determine the final guest count.
- Check with the florist to verify the delivery time and date for the flowers.
- Check with the other hostesses to see if all their tasks have been completed.
- Begin preparing your home for shower guests. Collect chairs and extra tables, dishes, and utensils from friends and neighbors.

Two days before the shower.
- Prepare the foods that can be completed ahead of time.
- Call the other hostesses as a final check to be certain that all is going well with their shower responsibilities.
- Check in with the bride, if it is not a surprise shower, to remind her of the upcoming occasion.

Day of the shower.
- Ask the other hostesses to arrive early in order to help you with the last-minute details.
- Decorate the area for the party.
- Set the tables and bride's gift area.
- Prepare foods.
- Take a deep breath and start answering the doorbell with a smile as the guests arrive.
- Ask guests to sign the guest book, if you have planned for one.
- Offer the guests a beverage.
- Wait for the bride. If it is a surprise, everyone will be anxious and concerned that the bride be caught unaware. Have someone be on the lookout for her. As she is arriving, hush the guests, and wait quietly and patiently. When she comes through the door, shout, SURPRISE! If the party is not a surprise, the guest of honor should still arrive after the guests. When she walks through the door, applaud.
- Pin a fresh-flower or satin corsage on the bride, praising her as the guest of honor.
- Let the bride spend approximately 15 minutes exchanging greetings with guests.
- Proceed with your scheduled plan as to eating and gift-opening.
- After the dessert is served, the guests will begin to leave.
- The bridegroom will arrive after the shower to help the bride take home the gifts and to eat some leftover food.
- The hostesses will clean up and muse about what a successful shower they gave.

Selecting
a Theme

Chapter 3

Selecting
a Theme

Focusing a shower on the bride's lifestyle begins with studying the bride. If one of the themes in this handbook fits your bride like a glove, then much of your planning is done. If not, then creating your own theme is simply a matter of answering some questions and using the tips that follow.

What is your bride's occupation? What hobbies or activities does she pursue? Is she interested in a specific type of decor? Does she enjoy any particular style of music? Is she a gourmet cook, a roller-skating enthusiast, or a theater buff? If she's a student, what is her major field of study?

Once you have identified the bride's lifestyle or have determined her interests, you're ready to develop the shower around a theme. If you need some ideas on a particular subject, check out some books from the library. As you will see in the discussion of the Victorian shower, the sonnets were taken from a research book. Also, books can be helpful in giving you background information to assist in preparing the decorations and food.

For example, if your bride enjoys photography, study some books on creative camera work. You can glean some good ideas for shower favors, decorations, invitations, and the wishing well. For the well, ask guests to bring a roll of film, album picture corners, or supplies for the bride's darkroom. A research book may identify specific pieces of equipment, and you can ask each invitee to bring something different.

For the bride whose consuming passion (besides her fiancé) is windsurfing, read books on the subject to help you understand what this water sport entails. If you know only a little about the sport, you may not be able to develop a theme around the bride's interest. You need not know everything about the activity. However, you should understand the subject to help inspire creativity.

If your bride doesn't have any abiding interest, hold a theme shower that complements the time of year. For example, if it is summer, have decorations, food, and invitations revolve around the warm season. If possible, hold the party poolside. If you do not know anyone with a private pool, summon your guests to a public pool or to the beach. (Be sure to ask the local pool and beach officials about the regulations regarding parties.)

No matter what theme you choose, you can mix and match decorations, recipes, and entertainment. For example, maybe your bride works in an office so you are giving her the Office Party At Home shower. But she is also very nutrition conscious. In that case, go to the section on A Shower Fit for a Healthy Bride, and switch the deli sandwiches to the Pita sandwiches.

As you sit with the other hostesses, dreaming up new ideas, you will find that establishing a theme is fun.

Name of the Bride: _____

Hostess(es): _____

Time of Shower: _____ Date: _____ Year _____

Place: _____

Theme: _____

1. Schedule of meetings to Plan the Shower: _____

_____

_____

2. Favors: _____

_____

_____

_____

3. Hostess Apparel: _____

_____

4. Invitations: _____

_____

5. Menu Notes: _____

_____

_____

6. Recipes: _____

_____

7. Gift Ideas: _____

_____

_____

_____

8. Wishing Well: _____

_____

9. Wishing Well Gift Ideas: _____

_____

_____

10. Entertainment: _____

_____

_____

NOTE: Indicate names in any section where someone has been as-signed to take care of a specific responsibility. Make photocopies of this work sheet and give one to each hostess at the first meeting.

Victorian Bridal Shower Is Steeped in Tradition

Chapter 4

Victorian Bridal Shower Is Steeped in Tradition

A return to romance and nineteenth-century splendor has prompted many brides to turn their weddings into fully frilly occasions. If your bride is interested in Victorianism, her shower should literally stop the clock circa 1890. This was the height of the Victorian period, which actually stretched from 1837 to 1901 while Queen Victoria reigned in England. It was an era of high fashion that encouraged our formal weddings today and perpetuated bridal customs such as throwing the bouquet to single women at the reception.

Victorian-influenced brides may buy a new nineteenth-century-inspired dress from a bridal shop, or they may wear their mother's or grandmother's wedding dress. They may also find a vintage wedding gown from an antiques shop. The wedding will probably be a formal one, so you might want to complement it by giving this stylish shower.

Decorations

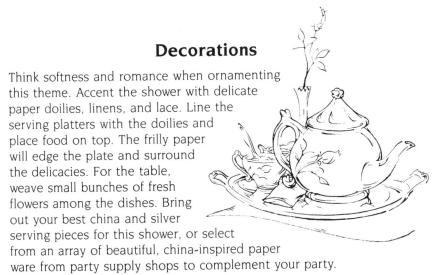

Think softness and romance when ornamenting this theme. Accent the shower with delicate paper doilies, linens, and lace. Line the serving platters with the doilies and place food on top. The frilly paper will edge the plate and surround the delicacies. For the table, weave small bunches of fresh flowers among the dishes. Bring out your best china and silver serving pieces for this shower, or select from an array of beautiful, china-inspired paper ware from party supply shops to complement your party.

Colorful nineteenth-century valentines, found at flea markets or antiques stores, can coax the romantic mood. Carefully string them together with grosgrain ribbon by punching a small hole at the top of the card (or post card) and knotting the ribbon before and after each card. Mount them across the gift table. Ask the antiques dealer for three-dimensional stand-up valentines to decorate your tables. The bride can later frame the old greetings and hang them as decorations in her new home. They will serve as constant reminders of her special friends and their thoughtful shower.

Favors

Stained glass was particularly popular during the Victorian period. Colorful glass sun-catchers—ones that literally reflect the theme, such as a high-button shoe—are possibilities for favors and are available from a stained-glass maker's craft shop. You can tie a printed ribbon containing the names of the bride and groom and their wedding date around the favor.

Another idea is to take a five-inch square of tulle (fine netting) and place two or three tablespoons of scented potpourri in the center. Gather the corners and tie with a printed ribbon.

Hostess Apparel

Hostesses may wear long skirts and high-neck collars accented with a cameo pin. If you don't have a long skirt, check your wardrobe for a long gown you no longer wear. Dresses formerly worn as bridesmaids costumes, for instance, may be turned into outfits for the Victorian shower. Usually the bodice of a bridesmaid's dress has that giveaway wedding party–style. Cut off the top and hem the waist, and you have a new skirt. Top it with a high-collared linen or flouncy blouse, and you will appear to have walked out of the nineteenth century.

Invitations

Paper doll cutouts are excellent bridal shower announcements for this theme. Some craft stores have books of Victorian paper cutouts. The cutouts include colorful pictures of nineteenth-century fashion for every occasion. Send each guest a different outfit.

Make the invitation by cutting out an article of clothing from the cutouts book—tabs and all. Then trace it on plain folded paper, placing the tabs at the top of the fold. Cut the design out, and then paste the real cutout on the front of the folded one. Write the announcement inside of the back fold. Buy envelopes to fit.

Entertainment

Aside from the opening of gifts, you might have a poetry reading, perhaps a few stanzas from love poems. Here are two:

Sonnet CXVI

Let me not to the marriage of true minds
Admit impediments. Love is not love
Which alters when it alteration finds,
Or bends with the remover to remove:
O, no! it is an ever-fixéd mark,
That looks on tempests and is never shaken;
It is the star to every wandering bark,
Whose worth's unknown, although his height be taken.
Love's not Time's fool, though rosy lips and cheeks
Within his bending sickle's compass come;
Love alters not with his brief hours and weeks,
But bears it out even to the edge of doom.
If this be error and upon me proved,
I never writ, nor no man ever loved.

William Shakespeare

The Passionate Shepherd to His Love

Come live with me and be my love,
And we will all the pleasures prove
That hills and valleys, dales and fields,
Or woods or steepy mountain yields.

And we will sit upon the rocks,
Seeing the shepherds feed their flocks,
By shallow rivers to whose falls
Melodious birds sing madrigals.

And I will make thee beds of roses
And a thousand fragrant posies,
A cap of flowers, and a kirtle
Embroidered all with leaves of myrtle;

A gown made of the finest wool
Which from our pretty lambs we pull;
Fair lined slippers for the cold,
With buckles of the purest gold;

A belt of straw and ivy buds
With coral clasps and amber studs:
And if these pleasures may thee move,
Come live with me and be my love.

The shepherds' swains shall dance and sing
For thy delight each May morning:
If these delights thy mind may move,
Then live with me and be my love.

Christopher Marlowe

The bride will adore these verses, and many guests will also appreciate hearing them. Make photocopies for interested guests who may want them as a keepsake.

Gift Ideas

Antiques make fine gifts for the Victorian bride. Here are a few other ideas related to the theme:

cameo pin
classic books from the Victorian era
decorative linens such as crocheted doilies
fabric lampshades
music box
ornate picture frames
padded hangers
sachets
subscription to a Victorian magazine
Victorian dolls

The wishing well for the Victorian shower can be a restored antique trunk, presented by the bridal party. Ask guests to bring fine old linens and not to wrap them. The day of the shower, display the delicate cloths by leaving the trunk open. If the trunk came with a tray, the linens will sit higher and be in better view than if tucked inside the deep crevice. Trunks were used as part of a Victorian's travel luggage. Place wishing well items into the trunk.

The Menu

Tea time, a Victorian institution, should be a highlight of this shower. There were two kinds of teas given by the Victorians. One was Regular Tea, the other, High Tea. Regular Tea was between 3 and 5 o'clock; High Tea was at 6 or 7 o'clock. Finger sandwiches, sweets, and of course tea, were served during Regular Tea. High Tea was more of a supper than an afternoon respite.

Regular Tea is really more practical for today. Schedule it for 1:00 p.m. On your invitation, call it a *Luncheon Tea Shower*. Guests will expect lunch and delicious, piping hot or refreshing chilled tea, depending on the season.

Decide on what teas to serve by consulting a gourmet shop that carries a full line of domestic and imported teas. Some teas are more suitable to a luncheon than others. Appropriate ones include Earl Grey and orange pekoe blends. Decide whether you want to serve with tea bags or loose tea, or both.

Loose tea is more traditional and elegant, but also more trouble. It may be better to serve with tea bags if you have a large group. An alternative to boiling pots full of water is to put loose tea bags in the filter of a drip coffee maker and follow the same procedures as if brewing coffee. The result is good, strong tea in a short amount of time.

Regardless of which method you employ, the hostess always serves the tea, and usually from her prettiest silver or ceramic tea-pots. (Cold tea may be poured from glass pitchers.) The correct way to serve the tea is to pour the cream in first and then to add the tea. Or, for spiced teas, serve with a slice of lemon, lime, or orange, and provide cinnamon sticks for stirring.

Have an alternate beverage on hand, such as Raspberry Mint Re-fresher, just in case one of the guest's palates has a distinct aversion to tea.

Sandwiches of cold meats and spreads are an easy yet attractive main course. Make them abundant but small. You can buy cocktail-size bread, or cut regular bread in half diagonally and in half again. Arrange the sandwiches on a platter in three or four layers. If you want to give the sandwiches color, have the bread dyed at a bakery. Line the sandwich platter with paper doilies.

To further encourage tradition, fill the sandwiches with Virginia ham. This was the festive meat of the nineteenth century, and it happened to be Queen Victoria's favorite dish. Add raw vegetables and dip to the menu. And, in keeping with tea-serving tradition, re-frain from offering anything that must be eaten with a fork.

The dessert should include a variety of sweets such as cookies, creme puffs, candy-coated almonds, sweet breads, nuts and fruit. You may also serve crumpets and scones with lemon curd or jellies. If you have a tea cart, by all means use it. Fill it with the desserts and roll it around to each guest, letting them choose among your fresh array of tasty treats.

During lunch, it's okay to have music playing softly in the back-ground, preferably classical melodies to complement the theme.

Recipes for the Victorian Shower

Queen Victoria Date and Nut Sweetbread

1 lb. dates, coarsely chopped
1 lb. pecans, coarsely chopped
¾ cup sugar
1 cup all-purpose flour
1 tsp. vanilla
2 tsp. baking powder
4 eggs

Preheat oven to 350 degrees. Butter an 8" × 4" × 2" loaf pan, and lightly dust with flour. In medium bowl, place the dates and pecans. Add sugar, flour, vanilla, and baking powder. Mix until blended. Add eggs, and continue stirring until batter is moistened. Pour the batter into pan. Bake one hour. Yields 1 loaf.

Prince's Poppy Seed Tea Cake

½ lb. softened butter
¾ cup sugar
4 egg yolks
¼ cup poppy seeds
2 cups cake flour
1 tsp. baking soda
1 cup sour cream
4 egg whites, stiffly beaten
1½ tsp. almond extract
1 tsp. cinnamon

Preheat oven to 350. Butter a tube pan, and lightly dust it with flour. Cream together butter, sugar, egg yolks, and poppy seeds. Sift together flour and baking soda, and then add to the butter mixture alternately with sour cream. Combine egg whites, almond extract and cinnamon and fold into the batter. Pour into tube pan. Bake for one hour. Cool on rack. Makes 10 servings.

Raspberry Mint Refresher

½ cup fresh mint leaves
1 cup boiling water
1 can (6 oz.) frozen lemonade concentrate
1 pint fresh raspberries, crushed and sweetened with ½ cup sugar
  (or one 10 oz. package frozen raspberries)
2 cups cold water

Combine ½ cup mint leaves and boiling water. Let steep 5 minutes. Add the raspberries and frozen lemonade concentrate. Stir (until thawed, if frozen raspberries are used). Pour into pitcher half-filled with crushed ice. Add cold water and stir. Makes 8 servings.

Doing Justice
to the
Legal Bride

Chapter 5

Doing Justice
to the
Legal Bride

The theme and ideas in this chapter are geared toward the bride-to-be who works in any aspect of law. She may be a judge, an attorney, a court stenographer, a secretary, or a file clerk.

Decorations

Brides who are in this category should be placed on a pedestal. Find a barstool or other high chair and have her sit behind a counter if possible, as a judge overseeing court. She can open her gifts in that position, allowing the guests to have a better view of what is inside each package. One of the hostesses should sit in a side chair as a witness with the responsibility to keep the gift tags with boxes and to prepare the paper bouquet.

A legal ledger should be used as the guest book. Ledgers are available in most stationery stores. Ask the guests to write their best wishes in legal puns such as ''Best wishes for a ticket to a long, happy marriage,'' or ''Congratulations on a lengthy courtship that is finally going to be legal.''

Place an American flag by the guest-of-honor's chair, and place a large Bible nearby to add to the atmosphere.

The wishing well may be a large Scale of Justice. You can borrow this symbolic statue holding two scales from a lawyer. Attorneys often have one of these statues decorating their offices. Some gifts will fit on the scale; arrange other gifts underneath it.

Favors

On a table next to the judge's perch, arrange miniature plastic gavels, one for each guest. Gavels are available at party supply stores. After purchasing them, cut six-inch squares of tulle (fine white netting) and fill each square with three tablespoons of rice, birdseed, or candy-coated nuts. Gather the four corners of the netting and secure them to the gavels with printed ribbon that includes the names of the bridal couple and the wedding date.

Hostess Apparel

To further complement the legal theme, the hostesses can dress in black robes similar to a judge. Black graduation gowns (without mortar boards) may be rented at a costume or graduation supply house and will really set the mood and distinguish the party hosts. You may want to have the bride dress in a white graduation gown.

Invitations

Prepare invitations to resemble a legal document, using legal transcription paper available at stationery supply stores. You might use this pronouncement:

You are hereby subpoenaed to witness the showering of gifts upon (bride's full legal maiden name). The bride's court will be held at twelve o'clock on the 12th day of April, (write out the year).

The honorable bridesmaids (list each name) will serve you at (insert address).

You are asked to testify on the bride's behalf by bringing an additional small gift, for the wishing well, with a legal connotation.

If you are unable to attend, please give notice to (name of hostess and phone number). Otherwise, we will expect to see you in court.

Buy envelopes to fit the invitations.

Entertainment

Have some fun with the bride by putting her on trial. Accuse her of not really knowing everything about her future husband and have her answer questions about her intended groom in order to be vindicated. A few days before the shower, call the groom and the groom's mother. Ask them for information about the groom's life. Try to gather the basic, detailed facts about his boyhood and growing years. Ask, for example, what year did he lose his first tooth? What was the name of his first girlfriend? When Halloween came around, how did he like to dress up?

You will be surprised at how much the bride does not know about her man. In fact, you will hear the other guests laughing and saying how stumped they would be if the same queries were made about their spouses. Develop at least 12 questions to make the quiz more interesting. The charges against the bride may be dropped if she answers correctly 6 out of 12 questions.

Have a court stenographer (or hire one) to record the entire shower and read it back after the gifts are all opened for more laughs.

Gift Ideas

Household items can be given as gifts, but ask guests to bring court-related paraphernalia for the wishing well. Here are a few possibilities: a set of red pens, yellow legal-size pads, a letter opener. Any desk supply that would be used in a legal office will also suffice. If the bridal party chooses to chip in for a wishing well gift, you may suggest a leather briefcase.

Menu

Almost any combination of foods will be conducive to this shower, but use an entrée cooked in parchment paper, and serve a courtly beverage. You might want to announce to guests, "Please come and get a cup of Truth or Consequences Punch and some chicken filed in legal paper!"

Recipes for the Legal Shower

Truth or Consequences Punch

1 can (12 oz.) of frozen lemonade
1 can (46 oz.) of unsweetened pineapple juice
1 fifth white wine
2 fifths inexpensive champagne
1 (10 oz.) package of frozen whole strawberries
ice cubes

Mix lemonade, pineapple juice, and wine in punch bowl. Just before serving, add ice, champagne, and strawberries. Makes enough to fill one punch bowl.

Legal Tender Chicken

1 boneless chicken breast half, skin removed
freshly ground pepper
2 Tbsp. ketchup
4 mushrooms sliced
Parchment paper available from kitchen supply stores

Place the chicken on a square piece of parchment paper. Sprinkle with pepper. Place ketchup and mushrooms on top. Fold and seal the parchment around chicken. Bake 15 minutes in 425-degree oven.

Make one chicken breast per guest. Bring all chicken breasts, still wrapped in paper, to the table. Have guests remove the paper and explain to them that the paper helps to seal in the juices and nutrients.

Serve the chicken with buttered spinach noodles, rolls, a cooked vegetable, and a garden salad.

Up, Up,
and Aloha:
A Honeymoon
of a Shower

Chapter 6

Up, Up, and Aloha: A Honeymoon of a Shower

Developing the shower theme around the honeymoon is one of the easiest decorating and planning schemes. This idea is for a couple going on an island sojourn. You can adapt it to almost any honeymoon location by using props appropriate to the post-wedding destination.

Decorations

Pay a visit to a travel agent and ask for posters depicting the honeymoon destination. The posters can be mounted temporarily around the room—the more, the merrier.

The shower area should reflect the feeling of a tropical island. Set indoor tree plants all around, and place fancy fresh flowers in large floor vases.

A piece of luggage, decorated with artificial flowers, can serve as the wishing well. The suitcase may be a joint gift from the bridal party, or you may use a second-hand one for this prop.

Favors

A nice way to greet your guests, and to later send them home with a shower souvenir, is to do what they do in Hawaii. Place a lei over each guest's head when she arrives. In Hawaii, the leis are often made from fresh flowers. But for the shower, just plan on buying plastic leis available at party supply stores. Have ribbons printed with the bride and groom's name and wedding date, and attach one to each lei.

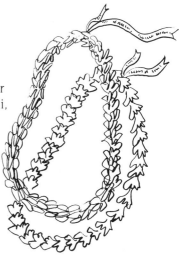

Hostess Apparel

Colorful tops over sarongs or grass skirts and sandals make comfortable, conducive costumes. Grass skirts may be purchased at party stores, or Polynesian outfits can be rented at a costume shop.

Invitations

Store-bought invitations will suffice for this shower. You may not find one specifically for showers, but a colorful, generic invitation that depicts an island motif will do.

Entertainment

Play Hawaiian music (records or tapes) in the background, and develop questions and answers for a trivia game, asking guests about geography and customs pertaining to the honeymoon destination.

You can also have a small troupe of hula dancers perform some exotic island dancing. Schedule them to appear after meal time and before the opening of the gifts.

Gift Ideas

Make the bride a whimsical Honeymoon Survival Kit. Ask the travel agent if you may have a few brochures depicting the area where the bride and her groom are going. Cut out portions of the pamphlets and glue them around an empty coffee can, covering the entire can. Fill the can with whatever small, whimsical items you think the couple will require on their honeymoon. Try to include only trinkets that allude to the honeymoon destination. For this shower, they might be a lei, a miniature oriental paper umbrella, a toy hammer to help open coconuts, and a pair of sunglasses.

Larger gifts can be luggage or traveling conveniences such as a traveling iron.

Menu

Set your table for a luau. Offer a few different dishes and decorate with fresh fruit and flowers between the platters. Guests will serve themselves, buffet style. The following is a suggested menu.

Snacks:	Cashew nuts
	Pineapple cheese ball served with bagel chips and raw vegetables
	Fresh pineapple chunks
Beverage:	Paradise Punch
Luau Entrées:	Tropical Chicken, South Seas Ham Delight
Side Dishes:	Tangy Pacific Spareribs
	Boiled White Rice
Dessert:	Fortune cookies with messages for the bride

Recipes for Up, Up and Aloha

Pineapple Cheese Ball
This cheese dip and spread can be made ahead of time and can be frozen until the shower.

2 cups pecans, chopped
16 oz. cream cheese, softened
1 (8½ oz.) can crushed pineapple, drained
3 Tbsp. red pepper, finely chopped
2 Tbsp. green onion, finely chopped

Using a fork, blend all the ingredients except 1 cup of pecans. Shape into ball and roll in the remaining pecans. Chill 2–4 hours. Serve with bagel chips and raw carrots, pepper, broccoli, and cauliflower.

Fresh Pineapple Chunks

1 whole pineapple
Red cherries
Colored toothpicks

Using a large sharp knife, cut the pineapple in half lengthwise. Cut in half again. Carefully slice the core lengthwise and discard. Separate the fruit from the rind and cut into chunks. Set the fruit on the pieces of rind and top with cherries and toothpicks.

Paradise Punch

16 large oranges
16 large lemons
2 cans (46 oz. each) unsweetened pineapple juice
2 cups sugar
2 cups water
6 bottles (29 oz. each) ginger ale
1 bunch mint leaves
1 pint fresh or frozen strawberries
Fresh flowers to float

Grate the rinds of 3 oranges and 3 lemons; squeeze juice from all the oranges and lemons and add the grated rinds and pineapple juice. Mix the sugar and water in a saucepan and bring to a boil, stirring until sugar is dissolved. Cool and add to juices. Add ginger ale, ice, mint, berries, and flowers. Makes one full punch bowl.

Tropical Chicken

6 whole chicken breasts (5 lbs.)
6 chicken legs and thighs (4 lbs.)
3 cans (1-lb., 1-oz. size) fruit cocktail
¾ cup soy sauce
1 clove garlic, minced
3 jars (8-oz. each) sweet-and-sour sauce

On the day before the shower: Preheat oven to 350. Wash the chicken; pat dry. Arrange, skin sides up, in a large shallow roasting pan.

Drain the fruit, reserving syrup. Pour the syrup and soy sauce over the chicken. Add the garlic. Bake, uncovered, basting often and turning chicken to brown all pieces, for 1 hour, or until chicken is rich golden-brown. Drain liquid into large saucepan.

Cover the pan of chicken tightly with foil. Add sweet-and-sour sauce to liquid. Bring to boiling over medium heat; boil until sauce thickens and is reduced to 3½ cups—about 40 minutes. Pour over the chicken.

Refrigerate, covered, along with drained fruit, overnight.

Day of the shower: About 1½ hours before serving, preheat oven to 350. Bake the chicken, uncovered, 30 minutes, basting often. Add fruit. Bake, 30 minutes longer, or until piping hot, basting several times. Makes 12 servings.

South Seas Ham Delight

3 cups cooked ham, diced
2 Tbsp. butter
1 can (13 oz.) pineapple chunks
2 medium green peppers, cut into strips
½ cup brown sugar
2 Tbsp. cornstarch
½ cup cider vinegar
½ cup chicken bouillon
2 tsp. soy sauce
1 Tbsp. whole cloves

Brown ham lightly in butter. Add pineapple with syrup and peppers. Cover and simmer 15 minutes. Mix sugar and cornstarch; add vinegar, bouillon, and soy sauce. Add to the ham mixture. Stir until thickened. Top with cloves. Makes four servings.

Tangy Pacific Spareribs

6 lbs. spareribs
1½ cups brown sugar
1 cup pineapple juice
1 cup crushed pineapple
½ cup prepared mustard

Place the ribs in baking dish. Combine all other ingredients and pour over the ribs. Bake, covered, basting occasionally, at 350 degrees for 45 minutes. Uncover and bake an additional 35 minutes. Serve with sauce. Makes 12 servings.

Fortune Cookies

Buy these from a grocery or Oriental food store. Insert tweezers into the cookie to pull out the slip of paper with the fortune. Cut separate papers to the same size and write your own good fortunes for the bride. Fold the papers and insert into the cookies. As each guest breaks open a cookie, she will read the bride a new fortune.

Messages may include:

You and (groom's name) will buy a house in two years.
You will find a buried treasure while on your honeymoon.
All of your guests will have the time of their life at your wedding.
Nothing will go wrong on your wedding day.

Be sure that any message you write, is happy, positive, and reflects good times ahead for the bride and her marriage.

Positive messages in cookies were the intent of the fortune cookie's inventor George Jung, an immigrant. In 1918, he wanted to cheer tired and war-torn residents of his new home, Los Angeles, so he took Bible verses and placed them into cookies. His company, Hong Kong Noodle Company, later enlisted someone to write 400 secular soothsaying messages to give patrons of Oriental restaurants something to think about while they waited for orders.

A Snow White
Shower
for the
Bride Who Skis

Chapter 7

A Snow White Shower for the Bride Who Skis

This shower is particularly appropriate, at any time of the year, for the bride who is an avid skier. Those who hug the slopes all winter do not seem to get enough of the white stuff. If it were up to them, they would schedule winter all year. A prewedding party with a skiing motif is the next best thing you can do for the bride who is basking in the sun but thinking snow. Bring the slalom sport to the bride even if it is 85 degrees!

Chances are the skiing bride will plan her wedding for the winter months so the honeymoon can be an escape to the slopes, or to the trails if she prefers cross-country skiing. If it is winter, try to hold the shower in front of a crackling fire to add atmosphere. If it is summer, consider holding the shower in an air-conditioned room.

Decorations

Mock lift tickets may be used for decorations by forming them into bows. First, have the tickets printed. Go to a printing shop and tell the printer you want to simulate a ski lift ticket. He can design such a ticket for you, using blanks similar to those at ski centers.

Select a color for the ticket that closely matches the shade of dress being worn by the bridesmaids. The tickets will also be used as the invitations to the shower.

To make the bows, gently fold the ticket in half without creasing. Staple where the two ends of the ticket meet. Do this with six tickets. Punch a hole in each ticket about one-half inch from the stapled ends. Take a white piece of yarn (about a foot long) and string the tickets together, forming a circle. Tie the yarn in a knot, and hang the whole unit from the ceiling.

Surround the bogus tickets by hanging paper or plastic snowflakes that you can buy in party supply stores.

Decorate the room where the shower is being held with greenery. The exact form of the decorations will depend on the shape of the room. Plastic evergreen trims used around the holidays can be hung to add to the outdoor scheme.

Favors

Party mementos that resemble a pair of crisscrossed skis will add to the decor at this shower. From a pharmacy or a surgical supply store, order a box of wooden tongue depressors as your skis. Paint them white. After they are dry, use a colored marker to draw a straight, thin line an eighth of an inch from the left edge and from the top to the bottom of the depressor. Turn the depressor horizontally in front of you. In small print, next to the line, write the bride's and groom's names and the wedding date.

Cross one depressor over another, placing glue at the point where the two depressors meet. It should resemble an X. Tie a piece of thin, colored satin ribbon (about eight inches long) where the depressors cross. The extra ribbon will allow the skis to be hung as Christmas tree ornaments or as seasonal decorations to remember the bridal couple.

Hostess Apparel

The bridesmaids can complement the decorations by wearing ski bibs if the weather is cool. If it is warm weather, bibs will be too hot. The hostesses can dress alike by wearing white outfits of their choice. In fact, ask the guests to dress in white clothing to complement the snow theme.

Invitations

Here again, you'll use the mock lift tickets. This time, they will be made into invitations to further enhance the skiing theme; Lift tickets are wide enough to include all the necessary information. Seek the printer's advice here. He'll guide you with typeface style and size. In addition to the usual party statistics, such as time and date of the shower, label the tickets *Unlimited Pass to (bride's name) Shower.* Put each into a properly fitted envelope, and mail.

Gift Ideas

Ask the guests to wrap all packages in soft white tissue paper, including the type of tissue paper studded with sparkles. Suggest that they fill the inside of the gift box with cotton balls instead of tissue paper to surround the gifts. The cotton can later be used by the bride for nonsterile applications. In the meantime, the cotton suggests snowballs. The package bows can be any color for contrast and interest.

As for what is placed inside the boxes, that can be up to the individual guests. Unless you know the bride needs ski accessories, do not suggest these items to guests. As a skier, the bride probably has all the essential equipment. Find out what she really does need. Maybe the bride and groom have one car ski rack and could use another. This is an item they probably would not buy for themselves, so it will be a welcome gift.

The decorations and menu will carry the theme without the inclusion of complementary gifts which the bride may have already. Since the suggested menu for the shower includes fondue cooking, you may want to be certain that someone gives the bride a fondue cookbook, fondue pot, a chafing dish, and pottery dishware.

Wishing-well gifts can reflect the theme. A large fireside basket is an appropriate wishing well for the bride who skis. Fill it with white tissue–wrapped items such as lip moisturizer, moisture cream, mirrored sunglasses, earmuffs, scarves, packets of facial tissues, candy mints, socks, a fanny pack (for food and accessories), a battery-powered foot warmer to heat frosty toes, and anything else you can think of which she might need on the slopes. The hostesses may combine their efforts and buy the bride a valid season's lift ticket for her favorite slope.

Wishing-well gifts can also include après-ski items such as a bottle of sherry, candles, assorted cheeses and crackers, hot chocolate mix, and fireplace matches in decorative cases.

Menu

Plan the menu around what the bride might look for after skiing. Basically, that's fruit juice, wine, or hot cocoa; cheeses, meat, crackers, and bread; and something sweet. Here are a few recommendations for the skiing shower.

Appetizers: Cheese mirror
Entrée: Beef fondue with French bread and raw fresh vegetables
Dessert: Yellow pound cake, fruit, nuts and hot cocoa

Recipes for Skiing Shower

Cheese Mirror

Place chunks of several different cheeses and dried sausage wedges on an unframed piece of mirror with toothpicks in each piece. Select imported cheeses from areas of the world where skiing is popular, such as Switzerland and Germany. Surround the mirror with curly lettuce. Complement the cheeses with an assortment of exotic crackers and garlic bread. Buy small flags representative of the country each cheese represents and place them in the cheese. The flags are reminiscent of a ski slope during some international competitions.

Classic Beef Fondue

Rent or borrow enough fondue pots for all of the guests, approximately one for every 6 people. This recipe serves 6 people per fondue pot.

2½ lbs. tender steak (at least one-inch thick)
    garlic powder
    wine vinegar
    dried onion flakes
    peanut oil
    fresh parsley
    Béarnaise sauce

The night before the shower, poke holes on both sides of the steak with a fork. Place in flat baking pan. Pour enough wine vinegar over the meat so that one side of the steak marinates. Sprinkle lightly with garlic powder and onion flakes. Refrigerate uncovered. After two hours, turn the meat and add garlic and onion to the other side. Keep repeating and turning (but not adding any more spices) every few hours. Cover overnight. On the morning of the shower, cut the meat into one-inch chunks. Return to the marinade and keep refrigerated, turning frequently on all sides.

On the day of the shower, follow the instructions for setting up your fondue pots. Place the guests at low tables. This arrangement is ideal for this type of serving. If low tables are not available, use card tables.

Place a fondue pot at the center of each table, half-filled with peanut oil. (Peanut oil does not burn as quickly as other oils.) In the meantime, place the chunks of meat on dishes and garnish with a few sprigs of parsley. Light the burners under the fondue pots just before guests are about to be seated. The oil will require about 10 minutes to heat through. Place a dish of meat on each table.

Note: Keep a fire extinguisher nearby. Although fondue pots are safe, accidents can happen when you are cooking with open flames. Baking soda also will smother flames.

When the oil is heated and lightly boiling, begin to fondue. Pierce a piece of meat with a fondue fork and set the fork into the hot oil. Let each piece brown slightly before removing. Dip it into Béarnaise sauce. Be certain there is a bowl of sauce for each table.

Après Ski Béarnaise Sauce

1 tsp. chopped onions
½ tsp. each of chopped fresh parsley and tarragon
12 peppercorns, crushed
2 Tbsp. dry white wine
1 Tbsp. wine vinegar
1½ cups margarine
5 egg yolks
2 Tbsp. light cream

Mix together onions, parsley, tarragon, peppercorns, wine, and vinegar. Simmer until mixture is reduced to one-half. Melt margarine and pour off the clear portion leaving behind the whey; the clear portion is *clarified* margarine. Beat egg yolks with cream. Beat vinegar mixture into egg yolks, and pour into the top part of a double boiler. Cook over boiling water until creamy.

While the sauce is cooking, beat constantly to avoid curdling. Gradually beat in the clarified margarine. Makes 1½ cups.

Raw Vegetables

Provide each table with fresh-cut vegetables as snacks while the meat is cooking. You can include broccoli, celery, cauliflower, carrot strips, radishes, cucumbers, and tomatoes. Serve with your favorite dip.

Dessert

The cheeses and the beef fondue are rich and filling food. Dessert should be simple. Cut small squares of your favorite pound cake and serve with nuts and fruits such as bananas, grapes, apples and pears (or fruits in season). A highlight of the skiing shower is a simmering cup of hot cocoa. Here is a recipe for serving a large group.

Skier's Cocoa

1¼ cups cocoa
1½ cups sugar
¾ tsp. salt
2 cups hot water
4 quarts whole milk
1½ Tbsp. vanilla
Small marshmallows

In a 6-quart saucepan, mix cocoa, sugar and salt. Slowly stir in water. Boil over low heat for 2 minutes, stirring constantly. Add milk, stir, and heat thoroughly. Do not boil.

Remove from heat. Add vanilla. Beat mixture with electric beater until foamy. Serve. Use a ladle to scoop the hot cocoa into mugs. Top each cup with a few small marshmallows. Makes 24 servings.

Saddle Up
the Trimmings
for the
Western Bride

Susan York   Ted Lind . June 17, 1988

Chapter 8

Saddle Up the Trimmings for the Western Bride

The bride who enjoys equestrian activities should be showered in a western motif. She may be an avid or an occasional horseback rider, or she may just have an affinity for horses. The theme can also be applied to the bride who is planning to honeymoon in a traditionally western ranching state.

Decorations

Colors will play an important part in decorating for this shower. The earth tones (brown, rust, dark green, and red) which you might see on a prairie or range, should dominate. Serve the food and drinks using paper plates and cups in these colors on a matching checkered linen tablecloth. Have guests sign their names in the white spaces on the checkered cloth with a fabric ink marker. Later, the bride can embroider the names as they were written and keep the tablecloth for use in her home.

Favors

Buy unpainted wooden rocking horse ornaments at a local craft supply store. If your
store doesn't carry the ornaments, ask the
proprietor to order them. Paint the horses
white and add a bow at their necks with
ribbon in the color of the bridesmaids' dresses.
Paint the bride's and groom's names and their wedding
date on the rocker part of the ornament. Slip a piece of the same
ribbon through the ornament's hanging loop. Display the favors on
a pegboard and place it by the bride's gift area.

Hostess Apparel

Jeans or denim skirts, topped with colorful gingham blouses and
scarves at the neck, will create a comfortable outfit for the hostesses.
Lasso the guests to dress the same way with a request in the invitation. Add that anyone wearing a cowboy hat gets an extra helping of
the goodies.

Invitations

Design a complementary invitation for this shower by selecting plain
stationery either in light blue (to suggest denim) or an earth-tone
color. Prepare the invitation as a note to a friend, in prose style. Use
color-coordinated envelopes.

Gift Ideas

The presents can be of a general nature, depending on the bride's
needs. Ask your guests to wrap their gift boxes in checkered cloth
napkins or bandanas, using double-sided tape, and securing the
package with ribbons. The bride will be able to reuse the fabric from
these wrappings.

Create a wishing well by building a small picket fence. Buy the fence sections from a garden center. Saw off the pointed bottoms, unless they're flat-bottomed stakes. Six or eight sections may be enough, depending on the number of guests. Place the sections in a square or rectangle and secure the sections where they meet in the corner. Stand the fence on the floor. Wishing well gifts may be placed inside the newly created corral.

A few ideas for this wishing well include barbecue tools, a country-western cookbook, vinyl tablecloths, saddle soap, horsehair brushes, neckerchiefs, and horseshoes.

Menu

You can hold a barbecue outdoors in warm weather. If it's too chilly outside, use a gas grill outside to cook your entrée. Remember, never barbecue indoors, as the fumes can be toxic.

The following menu is for an indoor party.

Appetizers:	Pottery spinach dip Sliced carrots, cucumbers, and celery Buttered popcorn
Beverages:	Apple juice Cranberry juice Grapefruit juice
Entrées:	Orange and honey chicken Baked pasta and cheese Prairie Vegetable Bake Old-fashioned baked beans Apple muffins
Dessert:	Spice cake

Recipes for the Western Shower

Pottery Spinach Dip

1 package (10 oz.) frozen chopped spinach, thawed and drained very
  well
½ cup scallions, finely chopped
½ cup fresh parsley, minced
2 cups mayonnaise
½ tsp. pepper
1 loaf unsliced round pumpernickel or rye bread

The day before the shower, combine all ingredients except the
bread. Hollow out the bread like a bowl, reserving bread cubes for
dipping. Just before guests arrive, place the spinach mixture into the
bread. Serve with bread cubes, carrots, cucumbers, celery, or other
raw vegetables. Prepare at least two of these dips, using rye bread
for one and pumpernickel for the other.

Orange and Honey Chicken

¾ cup bread crumbs
1 Tbsp. orange rind, grated
¼ tsp. pepper
1 chicken (3 lbs.), cut into pieces
½ cup orange juice
1 chicken bouillon cube
½ cup boiling water
4 Tbsp. butter
½ cup honey

Mix together bread crumbs, orange rind, and pepper. Dip each
piece of chicken in orange juice, then coat with the crumb mixture.
Place coated chicken on a lightly greased foil-lined 9" × 14" pan.
Store in the refrigerator. On the day of the shower, bake the chicken
at 350 degrees for 30 minutes. Dissolve the bouillon cube in boiling
water; add butter and honey. Stir until the butter melts. After the
chicken has baked 30 minutes, baste with honey glaze. Bake 35–40
minutes more, basting several times with the glaze. Makes 12
servings.

Baked Pasta and Cheese

1 package (16 oz.) shell macaroni
½ cup butter
½ cup flour
½ tsp. pepper
4 cups milk
4 cups (16 oz.) cheddar cheese, grated

Preheat oven to 375. Cook pasta as package directs. Meanwhile, melt the butter in large saucepan. Stir in flour and pepper and gradually add milk. Bring to boil while stirring constantly. Reduce heat. Simmer mixture 1 minute. Remove from heat. Immediately stir in 3½ cups of cheese. Pour 1 cup of the mixture into bottom of a large, shallow casserole or baking dish. Add the pasta. Pour remaining mixture into the casserole and stir until pasta is well covered. Sprinkle the remaining cheese over the top. Bake 15 minutes or until cheese is golden brown. Makes 12 servings.

Prairie Vegetable Bake

2 cups zucchini, sliced about ¼" thick
1 cup onion, thinly sliced
2 small tomatoes, sliced
⅓ cup dried bread crumbs
  pepper
1 tomato, cut in wedges
½ cup cheddar cheese, grated

In a 1½-quart casserole, layer half of the zucchini, onions, sliced tomatoes and bread crumbs, sprinkling liberally with pepper. Repeat the layers. Top with tomato wedges. Cover and bake 1 hour in 375-degree oven. Uncover and sprinkle with cheese. Return to oven until cheese melts. Makes 6 servings.

Knee-Slappin' Baked Beans

  4 cups navy beans
  ½ lb. fat salt pork
1½ Tbsp. brown sugar
  ¼ cup molasses
  ½ tsp. dry mustard

   Two days before the shower, wash the beans and soak overnight in cold water. The next morning, drain, cover with fresh water in saucepan and simmer until skins break. Turn into casserole dish or bean pot. Score the pork and press into the beans, leaving ¼" space above the beans. Add sugar, molasses, and mustard. Add boiling water to cover. Cover and bake in 250-degree oven for eight hours, without stirring, but adding water as necessary to keep beans covered. Uncover during last half hour to brown. Store in the refrigerator overnight. On the day of the shower, return the beans to the oven, cover and heat until warm enough to serve. Makes 8 servings.

Frontier Apple Muffins

  2 cups all-purpose flour
  4 tsp. baking powder
  ½ cup sugar
  ½ tsp. cinnamon
  1 egg
  1 cup milk
  1 cup unpeeled apples, chopped
  2 Tbsp. melted shortening

   On the day before the shower, stir the dry ingredients together in a medium bowl. In a separate bowl, beat the egg; add the milk, chopped apples, and melted shortening. Add to dry ingredients and mix lightly until blended. Fill two greased muffin tins ⅔ full, and bake at 425 for 20–25 minutes. Let cool. Wrap for storage. Just before serving, place the muffins in tinfoil and warm in oven (or microwave in suitable wrapping). Serve with the meal. Make sure you have enough servings, based on one muffin per guest.

Country Spice Cake

    2 cups flour
 ½ tsp. cinnamon
 ½ tsp. cloves
 ¼ tsp. ginger
    2 tsp. baking powder
 ½ cup shortening
    1 cup sugar
    2 eggs
 ¾ cup whole milk
    whipped cream

Two days before the shower, sift together the first five dry ingredients. Cream sugar and shortening, and beat in eggs until light and fluffy. Add milk alternately with the flour mixture. Bake in two greased 9" layer pans at 375 for 25–30 minutes. Let cool. Wrap in plastic and leave sitting out on a counter. On the day of the shower, cut into square pieces and serve with dollop of whipped cream.

For the Bride
Who Gardens

Karen
Bell
Mark
Collins
June 2, 1982

Chapter 9

For the Bride
Who Gardens

If puttering with soil and seeds, landscaping the backyard, growing fresh vegetables, caring for house plants, designing a flower bed, or nurturing an herb patch delights your bride-to-be, then consider giving her a garden shower.

Weather permitting, the shower should be planned for the garden. This setting could be in the backyard at someone's home or on a restaurant's lawn and patio banquet area. Be certain to have an alternate plan in case of rain or extreme heat or cold. Also, be prepared with tents (available for rent) to keep guests and food in the shade.

Decorations

Garden showers lend themselves to decorations provided by nature. The outdoor setting is all you need to create the mood. However, if the shower is indoors, be ready to cultivate some convincing gardening decorating schemes. The hostess's house will have to sprout greenery for this shower.

Real, artificial, and paper plants should be used to adorn the shower area. Any party goods stores will have an abundant supply of paper floral decorations and related items. In fact, this is one case where you can incorporate the traditional paper watering can into the theme shower. These three-dimensional cardboard-and-tissue cans come in varying sizes. You can mix them with some inventive designs of your own. For example, make a string of red tomatoes with construction paper if your bride is dedicated to the vegetable-growing portion of gardening. And/or create a lineup of connected, color construction-paper vegetables, and string them above the food table. Make these decorations yourself by drawing the vegetables on pieces of construction paper. Remember the folding cutouts you made as a child? Fold the paper several times, and cut around the penciled design. The finished product will open like an accordion.

Ask your guests ahead of time for cuttings from their favorite house plants. Offer to pick them up at their house a few weeks before the party. Use the cuttings to create newly potted plants, and place them around the shower area for the bride to take home after the shower.

Silk, dried, and fresh flowers can also be used to form centerpieces for the table and gift area. You can also have the bride sit under a halo of flowers by hanging a lightweight hoop from the ceiling over her chair. Attach dried flowers all around the hoop.

Favors

Purchase seedling-size starter pots from a garden center. Fill each with rice or birdseed, or use candy-coated almonds if the church does not permit the tossing of rice or seed after the ceremony. Cover the pot with netting, and fasten with a printed ribbon with the bridal couple's names and wedding date. Insert a small artificial flower in the center, and you have an appropriate favor for the garden shower.

Another type of keepsake also uses the seedling pots. A couple of weeks before the shower, fill them with potting soil and plant a seedling. Tie the same printed ribbon in a bow around the top of the pot. Each guest will take home a new living plant, just edging up past the soil and symbolizing the new life about to begin.

Hostess Apparel

Cool, casual, and comfortable describes the way the hostesses should appear at the gardener's party. Sport bibbed jeans, a checkered blouse, and a straw hat; or wear a patchwork shirt, a solid-colored skirt, and a bandanna. You may also mix and match the two by having some hostesses wear jeans and others wear skirts.

Everyone, including the guests, should wear a single flower corsage. Select either fresh or satin flowers in all different colors to add interest.

Invitations

You may use packaged, store-bought invitations for this shower. Find one with a garden theme. Remember, the term *shower* is associated with *April showers bring May flowers*, so plenty of invitations with floral motifs are available.

However, in the vein of the self-made invitation, plan something more creative. If you're having only a modest-size shower, consider sending each guest a single flower from the florist with a card inviting her to the event and including the pertinent information. An important consideration is that this can be more costly than standard invitations. Add up what it would cost you for printed invitations and postage, and decide whether this alternative is within your budget.

If this method is too costly, try another approach. Buy a packet of seeds for each guest—window sill plants for a bride who will live in an apartment, and outdoor garden or flower seeds for a bride moving into her own home. On plain white paper, write out the following message and place it with the seeds in an envelope:

We are planting the seed of a garden shower for (bride's name) that will bloom (date and time) at (location).

Enclosed is a packet of seeds. When nourished properly, the seeds will grow. Please start some for yourself and bring a pot with the seedlings as part of your gift to the bride.

Add any further shower information. Be sure to mention the wishing well if you are planning one.

Entertainment

Assuming the bride has been told she is having a shower, ask her to prepare a short lesson on her favorite type of gardening. Do not let on about the garden shower. Tell her she will find out soon enough what the request is all about.

For example, if she is an herb enthusiast, ask her to be ready to show her guests several herbs and to explain how they are used. Have her prepare recipe cards with medicinal and cooking recipes plus photocopies of the herb list she plans to talk about, in addition to the descriptions. Each guest can take a copy home for further study.

Gift Ideas

The gardening bride needs various tools to do her work, whether she plans to live in a house with land for gardening or in an apartment with only her window sill as her garden area. Do not underestimate the gardening opportunities for a bride who lives in an apartment. Some towns have a Rent-a-Garden program. For a slight fee, an apartment dweller can use a patch of soil in a designated area to grow crops. Your bride may intend to use that program. In that case, she may need heavy-duty garden tools. If she is unaware of such an arrangement, check with the county agriculture office where the bride will live. If the county does offer the growing patch, you may want to rent the soil as a gift to her.

A bride with her own house may need plenty of gardening supplies. Find out what she may need, and inform the guests prior to the shower.

A bride who is moving into an apartment can be given related items such as books on gardening, house plants, a plant stand and a colorful printed wall-hanging of a flower or garden scene.

In addition to the garden gifts, think of accessories such as a blender or food processor and canning jars to help prepare her home-grown produce recipes. Rakes, edgers, and cutting shears are also possible tools. Help the guests think up complementary gifts for the house, too. Floral sheets and bamboo or wicker picture frames are just two of many such items.

The wishing well should be a wheelbarrow bought by the hostesses, if the bride will live in a house. Use a borrowed one if she is going into an apartment.

Fill the wheelbarrow with garden-related items such as garden gloves, small planting tools, flower pots, and tomato cages.

Menu

Salad, deli meats, iced tea with fresh sprigs of mint, and fruit should comprise the menu.

Turn the main serving table into a salad bar. Place a huge bowl, full of three different types of lettuce, in the center of the table. Garnish it with grated carrots for color. Then surround the bowl with several small plates full of salad accompaniments such as green peppers, sliced onions, alfalfa sprouts, sliced raw mushrooms, tomatoes, olives, and cucumbers.

Serve cold cuts of ham, fresh turkey breast, and roast beef. It is less expensive to cook and slice the meats yourself. Also, offer a few varieties of sliced sandwich cheeses.

Prepare a watermelon full of fresh fruits for dessert. Cut the melon in half lengthwise. With a melon scooper, carve out melon balls and set the fruit aside. When the melon is completely removed from the rind, load the shell with the melon balls plus grapes, strawberries, pineapple, blueberries, and other fruits in season.

Salad Dressing Recipes for the Garden Shower

Cider and Cream Dressing

1 tsp. salt
1 Tbsp. sugar
⅛ tsp. cayenne
1 Tbsp. fresh lemon juice
2 Tbsp. apple cider vinegar
1 cup sour cream

Combine all ingredients. Makes 1 cup.

Verdant Earth Dressing

1 cup mayonnaise
½ cup chili sauce
2 Tbsp. minced green pepper
3 Tbsp. chopped green stuffed olives
1 tsp. grated onion
2 tsp. chopped chives

Combine all ingredients. Makes 2 cups.

Down-to-Earth Cheese Dressing

½ cup Roquefort cheese, crumbled
3 oz. cream cheese
½ cup heavy cream
½ cup mayonnaise
1 Tbsp. fresh lemon juice
1 Tbsp. wine vinegar

Blend the Roquefort and soft cream cheese. Beat in cream. When blended, stir in the mayonnaise, lemon juice, and vinegar. Makes about 1¼ cups.

French Soil Dressing

½ cup fresh lemon juice
1½ cups olive oil
¼ tsp. pepper
1 tsp. powdered mustard
2 garlic cloves, finely minced

Mix all ingredients in a 1-quart jar; cover tightly and shake until well blended. Makes 2 cups.

An Office Party at Home

Chapter 10

An Office Party at Home

The boss is not around. There are no water coolers to chat by . . . no coffee machines for an unscheduled meeting. No men are allowed. This is a party for women only—a shower for the bride who works in a business or corporate environment all day. She may be a file clerk, typist, secretary, keypunch operator, receptionist, administrative assistant, department manager, vice president, chief financial officer, company president, computer specialist or programmer, CEO, or in any other company position. Before selecting this theme, make sure you know that the bride is content with her job.

Decorations

Create an office atmosphere at home. Have the bride open her gifts behind a desk. Decorate the top with a blotter, telephone, pen and holder, and vase of fresh flowers.

On a wall behind her, hang a large bulletin board. On one area of the board, randomly post shower wishes from the people in the bride's office. Obtaining these notes may require an extra effort on your part. You may have an advantage, being close to the bride, and knowing some of her working colleagues. Call them and ask them to write short messages, jokes, or anecdotes about the bride. Pin them on the board.

During the opening of the gifts, take the greeting card accompanying the gift and post it on the bulletin board. The result will be a colorful array of wishes for happiness. However, in order to keep track of who gave the gift, quickly write the name of the gift-bearer on an index card and slip it in with the gift. You're simply making an exchange of gift identification.

Check with a local office supply store for premade decorations. Some have three-dimensional cardboard versions of a computer and keyboard. Ask if they have any extras that you could use for one day. Place one cardboard computer on the bride's desk and any others that are available in various places around the room.

Decorate the walls with motivational posters. You can buy them in card shops and stationery supply stores. Choose colorful posters with appropriate messages such as, one of my favorites, one depicting a bunch of docked, old dinghies with the message *Captains of great ships begin here.*

In the center of the table, place an artfully decorated shower cake. A layered sheet cake, designed to resemble a typewriter, will make an ideal centerpiece. Ask people in your neighborhood for the name of someone who bakes and decorates cakes to suit an occasion, or ask the local baker to design a typewriter or computer keyboard with icings.

Place small floral arrangements on the food table and in other sections of the shower area to soften the strictly business appearance.

Favors

Purchase the colorful, pocketbook-size yearly date books for each guest. Record the bride's and groom's birthdays and wedding date in the appropriate sections in the book. Some stationery stores can arrange to have the outside covers of the date books imprinted in gold with the names of the bride and groom and their wedding date. Ask the store if this is possible, and decide whether it fits into your budget. It may be less expensive just to have ribbons printed as bookmarks that can be used with the date book.

Another favor idea is to make something complementary of the shower theme that can later be tossed over the newlyweds. Fill envelopes with white paper confetti (to throw instead of rice). Make the confetti by punching holes in the paper. (Do *not* use colored paper, as it may bleed onto clothing on a hot day.) Seal the envelope, and tie a ribbon, printed with the couple's names and wedding date, around it. The confetti will be tossed over the bride and groom as they leave the church after the wedding ceremony. Before you create this favor, ask someone to be responsible to sweep the area as soon as the nuptial couple leaves for the reception. Offer this cleanup help to the minister or other official when you ask if throwing the confetti is permissible outside of the house of worship.

Hostess Apparel

Slacks and a jacket with a button-down blouse and man's business-style tie make ideal costumes for this shower. They are comfortable and create the business scene.

In the spirit of a corporate meeting and luncheon, buy "Hello My Name Is" self-stick tags, and have all the guests wear one. Inscribe their names before the day of the shower.

Invitations

Send friendly, business-like invitations. If the bride works with a computer during the course of her day, print the invitations on computer paper (with the holes on the sides). If possible, use a dot-matrix printer, as the type produced by this machine definitely implies the beckoning card was done on a computer.

Write a clever message such as this:

Our company (list names of hostesses such as Jones, Smith & Brown, Inc.) is holding a special shower luncheon for employee (name of the bride) on (date and time of the party) at (location).

We hope you can be there to watch the bride work at her desk.

A file cabinet will be on hand to receive your wishing-well gifts.

Our Company, Jones, Smith & Brown, Inc,
is holding a special shower luncheon for
employee, Barbara Samson on June 15, 1988,
2:00 at 2654 Lane Rd,
We hope you can be there to watch the
bride work at her desk,
A file cabinet will be on hand to receive
your wishing well gifts

If the bride is not involved with computers, make the invitation a memo. Buy a pad that has *Memo* printed on it in large letters. Type the invitations below the letters. Use the same wording as for The computer bride. Fold. Place into an appropriately sized envelope for mailing.

Gift Ideas

As mentioned in the sample invitation, a file cabinet can serve as the wishing well. The cabinet can be borrowed or purchased as a gift from the hostesses to the bride. You can also use In and Out baskets for the wishing well. Place small items into the basket you label In. As the bride opens each gift, she will place it into the basket labeled Out.

When guests call in their invitation responses, ask them to wrap their gifts in office paper—clean lined pages or colored bond, and have them top the packages with colorful bows.

Gifts may include household items, or you may suggest office supplies for the bride's house or apartment. If you know she intends to have a desk at home, suggest these gift ideas to help her get started. Some items may be considered the main gift, others are suitable for the wishing well.

answering machine
blank computer disks
blotter
bookends
box of manila file folders
business magazines
computer paper
desk calculator
desk calendar
desk lamp
desk nameplate
dictionary
in/out baskets
memo pads
paper clips
pencil sharpener
phone/address book
portable radio
postage scale
rotary address file
scissors
scotch tape
typing paper
wall calendar

Menu

Encourage the office atmosphere with a water cooler filled with a fruit juice, punch, or other beverage of your choice. You can rent or borrow a cooler. Guests can refill their own glasses, getting to know each other at the water cooler just as they would do in an office.

Many times when we are too busy to go out for lunch, we call up for a sandwich to be delivered to the office. Do the same for this shower by creating the illusion that nothing was prepared ahead of time.

And, in fact, perhaps you have not prepared anything. If your shower budget provides, have this party catered. Just as you would send out for sandwiches to be delivered to the office, arrange for caterers to send over sandwich platters.

If funds are limited, you may arrange the platters yourself with a variety of meats and salads. However, since you want to create the office "send out for lunch" illusion, you will have to prepare these platters in someone else's home on the morning of the shower.

In addition, in advance order all types of breads, and arrange to pick them up at the bakery. Place the breads in baskets. The more types of bread, the better, including French, Italian, onion rolls, bagels, whole wheat and granola breads, rye and pumpernickel, and sesame seed buns. Store these at the same house where you plan to keep the platters.

Store the condiments in your own refrigerator. Salad dressings, mustard, ketchup, and any other sandwich fillings such as pickles, onions, and olives can be at your house. Include potato chips and a few dips, plus cut raw vegetables.

Arrange in advance for a couple of friends to deliver the goods when it is time to eat. Preset that time so that they will know when to arrive with the food. This is how you do it to create the illusion you are calling out for lunch:

Make a bogus phone call in front of the guests, and speak loudly so all of them can hear. State into the phone: "I would like five platters of cold cuts, 60 rolls, 20 loaves of bread," and so forth. Specify each item on the menu. Refer to a written list so nothing is forgotten. The idea is to make the call seem as realistic as possible. Remember to leave your name, address, and phone number. Conclude the phone order with this, "Can you deliver it right away, please?"

Everyone will have fun trying to guess what is going on. When the food arrives, the guests will be delightfully surprised. As your friends march in, their arms weighed down with overflowing bread baskets and food platters, announce to everyone, "It's time to break for lunch."

This
Bridal Shower
is Sew Special

Chapter 11

This Bridal Shower Is Sew Special

Any bride who knows how to sew will appreciate this shower. She need not be a full-time seamstress, just someone who would rather hem her own skirt and pants than take them to a tailor. Or sewing might be her favorite pastime, and she enjoys creating clothing or things for around the house.

Decorations

Create a sewing room environment. Hang spools of thread and bows. The length of this decoration will depend on where you hang it—either across the room or along the side of the main table. Using fabric piping, string two spools and then tie a bow. Repeat the design for the desired length. Use large spools in the center and small ones toward the ends. When the shower is over, the bride gets to use the thread (which may last her entire married life), the piping, and the bows.

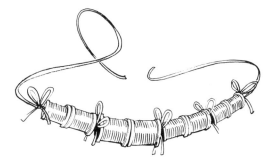

In another area, you can hang antique wooden spools with bias tape. Thread today is wound around plastic spools. But in the past, they were wooden. Ask friends to search their attics for old-fashioned spools. Have a painting party with the rest of the attendants or the other hostesses. Paint the spools different colors. If someone is artistic, have her accent the spools with blossoms. (If you cannot find wooden spools, use the plastic or foam ones.)

Then, take bias tape and cut it at different lengths. Hang the spools at the bottom by knotting them to the seam binding. These decorations are hung from the chandelier over the table. As an alternative, decorate an umbrella. Choose one that closely resembles the color of the bridesmaids' dresses. Select a complementary shade of seam binding, and cut two-inch long streamers. Cut one streamer for every spoke. Take an empty wooden spool and knot it to the other end of the streamer. Do this for every spoke. Then hang the umbrella over the bride's chair, with the handle facing the wall. You could also hang it upside-down from the ceiling.

If you can find the larger, commercial wooden spools, set them out on tables, and place a lighted candle in each. These antique spools are commonly used today as candle holders. They are available in antiques shops.

Favors

Miniature scissors-holders filled with rice, birdseed, or candy, tie in nicely with this theme. See the instructions later in this chapter for making the holders. Here's how to make the bundles of rice, seed, or candy to place in the holders: Put about three tablespoons of rice in the center of a five-inch square of tulle. Gather the ends of the netting. Then bring the netting together, and tie with a satin ribbon printed in gold with the name of the bride and groom and their wedding date. Place a bundle in each scissors holder, and distribute the favors to the guests as they leave. Tell them they can mount the holder in their own sewing room and keep lightweight snipping or manicure scissors in it.

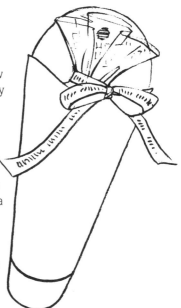

Another favor suggestion makes good use of old buttons. Make a bundle of buttons by collecting all of the old buttons you can find. Fill a five-inch square of white netting with about two handfuls of buttons. Tie the bundle with a printed ribbon displaying the names of the bridal couple and their wedding date. Insert one small silk flower between the netting and ribbon.

Hostess Apparel

Dress comfortably for this shower. Have the hostesses wear slacks and colorful aprons. Ask guests to wear garments they may have sewn.

Invitations

Make use of sewing notions as part of the invitations. The following is a suggestion that uses buttons, sequins, and lace trim.

You will need these materials to complete the invitations:

Blank note cards that open out to 3¾" × 4¾"
Flat light-colored pink buttons, about ¾" in diameter, with two center holes in each
White felt (or colored)
White lace (about 1" wide)
Assorted felt-tip pens
Craft glue
White sequins, about ½"

Write details of invitation inside card. Begin completing outside front of card by gluing a button to the card, with the center of it approximately two inches from bottom of the card. Tilt it slightly so the buttonholes are askew. Be sure not to use too much glue, as it will saturate the card.

Cut out felt by tracing the outline of a hat. Cut out three layers of lace, graduating in size so each piece totally covers an area of felt. Glue them to the felt.

With black felt-tip pen, make two lines for a neck. (See illustration.) With red felt-tip pen, draw small lips. If pen does not stick, use a paintbrush and watercolor paint.

With felt-tip pen of your choice, draw hair as indicated in the illustration on page 87. Glue sequins below hair, where earrings would fall. Finish by drawing the top of an *m* below the lines that make the neck.

HAT PATTERN

Entertainment

Have a sew-in for fun and as part of the gift-giving to the bride. If your guests number 20 or fewer and most of them know sewing basics, this will work out well. Supply precut fabric in the shapes of aprons, potholders and napkins. You and the other hostesses will have to cut out the pieces for these ahead of time.

Ask each guest to bring her own sewing basket of notions and threads and a portable machine, if she has one. Borrow card tables, and set two guests at each one. Let them select either an apron, potholder, or napkin kit and let the threading begin.

This will take about an hour and a half. The results will be plenty of new kitchen accessories for the bride.

Gift Ideas

Since this bride probably has the basic tools for her craft, it's better to present her with household gifts. However, the bridal party or the hostesses might chip in for a combined gift such as a dress form, a sewing cabinet, or a new sewing machine. These are gifts the bride may like to have but probably would forego at this time.

Ask guests to wrap their presents in fabric. Use double-stick tape to fasten the fabric to the package. Then give the package added security by fastening it with complementary ribbon. The bride can re-use the fabric.

The wishing well can be a sewing basket. Ask guests to bring small items such as packages of buttons, pins, hooks and eyes, safety pins, needles, and other sewing notions. The bride may have most of these, but they are the kind of seamstress supplies she can always use. The hostesses may chip in and buy an advanced sewing how-to book to complement the wishing well.

Menu

Because of the unusual nature of this shower, it should be scheduled after lunch. Serve only snacks and beverages during the sewing. Let the bride open the other gifts afterward, and conclude the shower with cake and coffee.

Directions for Scissors Holder Favors

Supplies
Heavy cardboard
Spray paint
Craft glue
Netting
Rice
Satin ribbon

Using cardboard, cut pieces as indicated by the pattern. Spray paint (your choice of color) all pieces. After the paint has dried, attach sides with glue and let the glue dry. Place the front of the holder on the sides, and glue. When the glue is dry, the holder is complete.

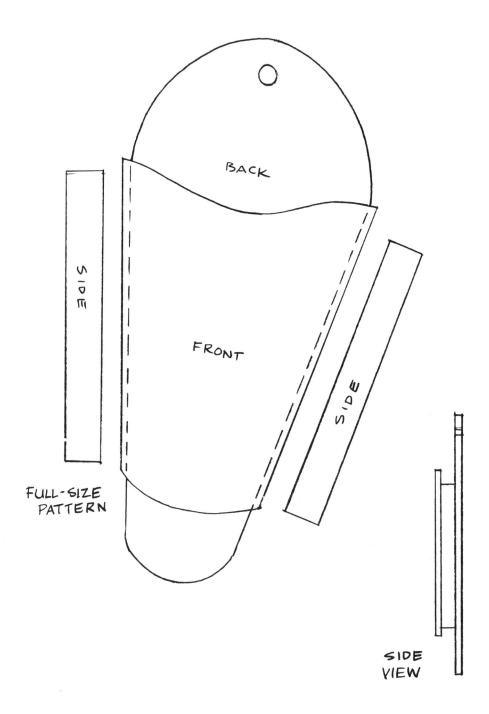

BACK

SIDE

FRONT

SIDE

FULL-SIZE
PATTERN

SIDE
VIEW

90

A Country Shower
for the
Early American
Bride

Chapter 12

A Country Shower for the Early American Bride

What do sheep, teddy bears, pineapples, and old quilts have in common? If they're handcrafted imitations of the real thing, they fall into the category of folk art. And if the bride is interested in Country decor, she knows immediately what the barnyard animals, stuffed toys, wooden fruits, and hand-stitched comforters symbolize. She probably intends to accent her home with these accessories. Designing the shower around the bride's personal decorating style, whether it is Country, contemporary, traditional, or early garage sale, will delight her.

Many new brides are planning Country homes. Your question may be, "But just what is *Country*?" You certainly need to know if you are going to create her shower around this theme. Country is a decorating mode that reflects rural life during America's toddling years. Architects and interior designers say Country, which surfaced in the late 1970s, is here to stay, as is its other side, the more formal Colonial decor.

Country is often confused with Western. It is not of the Hee-Haw variety. Country means primitive, Early American antiques, collectibles, and stenciling. A Country-accented home paints a primitive picture with its plain furniture and accessories. Shaker and Amish styles also fall into this category. Country decor is popular because it reminds a high-tech society of quieter times. The look is captured in city apartments as well as remote farmhouses.

To plan this shower, you need to think simplicity—folksy and rustic. Browse through Country magazines for clues as to Country's identity. The magazines, plus Country decorating and collecting books, will help you better understand this type of decor.

Decorations

Baskets play a large role in decorating a Country bride's home. Do the same for her shower. The older the basket, the more the Country bride will like it. Old baskets are available at antiques stores (warning: antique baskets can be costly). A Country bride also appreciates new baskets. Remember, you can also borrow baskets. Place the baskets all around the shower area. The larger ones can rest on the floor. You may fill them with an assortment of dried flowers.

Decorate the walls with grapevine wreaths and Country straw bonnets adorned with dried flowers and ribbons. These and other Country trinkets can be found at craft boutiques or fairs.

Set a number of candles out and burn them instead of electric lights.

An hour before guests are to arrive, start simmering spiced pot-pourri on the stove. The sweet scent will add to the Country atmosphere. Potpourri packets are available in craft shops and gourmet stores. You can make your own by filling a four-quart saucepan about three-quarters full with water. Add one-half of an orange and one-half of an apple. Pour in one-half ounce each of cinnamon, nutmeg, allspice, and cloves, and bring to slight boil. Lower the heat and leave simmering. Continue adding water to the pot as the level decreases (about every hour).

Favors

Miniature Country baskets will send guests home with a fond remembrance of the Country shower. Purchase the tiny baskets at craft supply stores. Place a tied netting of tulle, filled with rice or birdseed, into the basket. The favor will provide guests with a keepsake and a handy caddy for carrying their rice or birdseed to the wedding.

Another favor requires slightly larger baskets. Fill each basket with other Country articles such as a sweet-smelling bag of perfumed potpourri or handmade soap. An even larger basket can hold a small bottle of wine, cheese, and crackers. Whichever basket favor you choose, be sure that the names of the bride and groom and their wedding date are printed on a ribbon and tied in a bow around the handle of each basket.

You can also use teddy bears for favors. Buy small stuffed bears (no larger than four inches high). Secure a printed ribbon displaying the bridal couple's names and wedding date around the bear's neck. Your guests will love it no matter what their ages.

Hostess Apparel

Hostesses can wear prairie dresses or skirts and fabric bonnets similar to those worn by the Amish and Shaker women today. Or, if you and the other hostesses have modern clothing that reflects the Country look, let everyone dress individually. There are Country-inspired sweaters, for example, that have farm animals woven into their designs.

Invitations

Invite the bride to her shower in the spirit of colonial times. Check in your area to see if there is a service that delivers telegrams by way of costumed couriers. If so, they probably can send someone dressed as a town crier, circa 1776. Dressed in colonial garb such as a tricornered hat, brass-button jacket, knickers, and boots, he will arrive at the bride's door, calling out the shower invitation that you have prepared.

To prepare the shower information the crier will deliver, have someone who is adept at calligraphy write the message on brown parchment paper. Then roll it up as a scroll. As the crier reads the message, he will unroll the paper in front of the bride, not unlike a messenger might have done in colonial days. He will then reroll the parchment, and hand the bride her invitation.

If you are not near such a service, ask a male friend to be the patriotic messenger. Rent a colonial statesman's outfit for him from a costume shop.

Invite the guests with stenciled WELCOME signs. (See directions later in this chapter.) The shower information will be written on the back. The sign is designed with a paper stand so that it may sit on a counter or table and remind the invited guest of the upcoming event. These signs, much larger and carved from wood, are a common item in a Country home.

Gift Ideas

When you devise a list of various gifts for the Country shower, think of everyday household items that were used in someone else's home more than 50 years ago. For example, instead of buying the latest pressing iron, go to the antiques shop for an old iron that was originally heated with charcoal over an open fire. Your bride will use the antique iron in her home as a heavy doorstop or decorative bookend. An accompanying gift could be an old wooden ironing board, fastened with wooden pegs. They are used in Country homes today as tables located in front or in back of a sofa.

In addition to antiques, the Country bride will appreciate almost any item that is homespun. Shop in craft boutiques for accessories that she can use in her home such as a duck decoy, pierced-tin wall hanging, or an Amish doll that has no facial features, in keeping with the Amish faith.

Ask each guest to wrap her gift in Country-style wrapping paper, identified by its small prints and warm colors. These prints are available in most full-line card shops.

A gift certificate for a night at a Bed and Breakfast Inn would make another exciting gift for this bride. These facilities provide old-fashioned lodging and are located all over the country and in Europe. Find the one nearest to where your bride will be living.

The Country bride's wishing well should be a wicker laundry basket filled with all types of kitchen tools, from a nutcracker to a lemon squeezer. Ask your guests to look for unusual items the bride probably would not buy for herself.

Instead of recipe cards for this shower, ask guests to write tried-and-true household hints and old-fashioned medicinal remedies on cards. Have one of the hostesses read each guest's suggestion out loud after the opening of the gifts. Have a basket on hand to receive the cards. As each guest arrives, be certain she places her card in the basket.

Menu

Open-hearth cooking was familiar to the colonists, settlers, Indians, and prairie travelers. Country and Early American enthusiasts still continue open-hearth cooking today as a pastime. If you know how to use this cooking method, then by all means give your guests a treat. Most of us, however, due to a lack of equipment—including having a giant cauldron handy—can only hope to duplicate the process and sample a taste of the past by serving entrées similar to those our pioneers prepared.

The menu for this shower is old-fashioned beef stew, country corn pudding, Paul Revere (cheese) muffins, and Colonial baked apples. Serve the stew in a black kettle to encourage the down-home atmosphere. Set it at the far end of the table. The hostess will scoop stew by the ladle-full into each guest's bowl.

Recipes for the Country Shower

Old-Fashioned Beef Stew

  2 lbs. beef chuck, cubed
  3 Tbsp. all purpose flour
  3 Tbsp. shortening
  ¼ tsp. fresh-ground pepper
  6 cups water
 12 small white onions
  2 cups zucchini, diced
  6 carrots, peeled and cut into chunks
  4 medium potatoes, peeled and cut into quarters
  1 celery stalk, cut into one-inch pieces

Dip the meat into the flour, covering all sides. Melt shortening in kettle. Add the meat, and brown on all sides. Add pepper and water. Bring to a boil; simmer, covered for 1½ hours or until meat is almost tender. Add remaining ingredients, and simmer for 45 minutes. Makes 6 servings.

Country Corn Pudding

  2 packages (10-oz. size) frozen corn, thawed and drained
  3 eggs, beaten
  2 tsp. onion, grated
  ¼ cup all-purpose flour
  ½ tsp. pepper
  1 Tbsp. brown sugar
    dash nutmeg
  2 Tbsp. butter, melted
  2 cups light cream
  1 can (4 oz.) pimentos, drained and coarsely chopped

Preheat oven to 325 degrees. Lightly grease a 1½-quart shallow baking dish. In a large bowl, combine corn, eggs, and onion; mix well. In a small bowl, combine flour, pepper, sugar, and nutmeg. Stir into corn mixture. Add butter, cream, and pimentos; mix well. Pour into prepared dish. Set the dish in pan. Pour hot water in to 1" depth around dish. Bake uncovered 1 hour or until pudding is firm and a knife inserted in the center comes out clean. Cut into squares and serve hot. Makes 8 servings.

Paul Revere Muffins

1¼ cups buttermilk
1 cup whole bran
4 Tbsp. shortening
⅓ cup sugar
1 egg
1½ cups flour, sifted
1½ tsp. baking powder
¼ tsp. baking soda
1 cup cheddar cheese, shredded

Place bran in a small bowl and pour the buttermilk over it. Let stand until bran softens. Cream shortening and sugar until light and fluffy. Beat in the egg. Sift together flour, baking powder, and baking soda. Add to creamed mixture alternately with milk-bran mixture. Stir in the cheese. Fill greased muffin pans ⅔-full. Bake at 375 for 25–30 minutes. Makes 18 muffins.

Muffins can be made ahead of time and frozen. Defrost, and, just before serving, wrap them in tinfoil. Warm in the oven and serve.

Colonial Baked Apples

6 large baking apples
¾ cups of sugar
½ cup unsweetened apple juice
2 Tbsp. butter
2 Tbsp. light brown sugar
1 tsp. ground cinnamon
2 Tbsp. fresh lemon juice
1 Tbsp. sliced almonds

Core the apples, but do not pierce the bottom of the fruit. Make core opening about one-inch across, for the filling. Place the apples in a baking dish with a little space between each one. In a small saucepan, combine the juice and sugar; heat to boiling. Stir lemon juice into the syrup. Pour syrup over the apples, but not too much into the cores.

In small bowl, combine butter, brown sugar and cinnamon. Fill the cavity of each apple with almonds. Top each with some butter mixture.

Bake apples at 350 for 45 minutes or until tender. Baste occasionally with syrup. Serve warm. Makes 6 servings.

Directions for Country Shower Invitations for the Early American Bride

Welcome signs like the one shown on page 96 are often displayed in Country and Early American homes. They usually are made of wood and are decorated with stenciling or tole painting. The pineapple is often part of the sign, since it has long been the symbol of welcome. Your invitation can also be displayed in your guests' homes before the party. This invitation is designed to stand on a flat surface, so it will be a decorative reminder of the upcoming shower.

Making this invitation will give you the experience of stenciling, an old art that is coming back.

You will need the following supplies:
Pencil
Scrap paper
Stencil (provided here)
Pen
Paint (brown, green) acrylic
Poster paper
Envelopes (6½" X 3½")
Two natural sponges
Ruler
Glue
Artist's knife and/or scissors

1. Draw a 6" straight line on a piece of paper.
2. Make a small dot in the middle of the line.
3. Measure and draw a 2" straight line up from the dot.
4. Form a half-circle with your pencil over the 6" straight line. The top end of the 2" line is the largest part of the half-circle.
5. Cut out the half-circle, and trace onto the poster paper for each invitation.
6. Cut out the pineapple using the pattern provided. This is a small stencil. Place the pattern in the middle of the half-circle. Take a small sponge and dip it into your brown paint. Remove the excess paint by dabbing the sponge on a white paper plate. When you stencil, you should use as little paint on your applicator as possible.
7. Gently dab the sponge on the stencil. Lift the stencil, and the pineapple imprint will be there.
8. Stencil all of the pineapple bottoms.
9. With the other sponge, stencil the tops of the pineapples using the green paint.

10. Now write your welcome (such as *Welcome to Brenda's shower*) on the front side of the invitation.

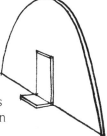

11. To make the invitation stand up, cut a piece of poster paper 1" long × ½" wide. Glue the piece on the back of the invitation, allowing ¼" hanging over the invitation. Fold the excess ¼" of paper up, and then lay flat. The invitation now has a support to lean on.
12. Write the pertinent shower information on the back, writing around the stand.
13. Place the welcome invitation in the envelope, and it is ready for mailing.

STENCIL PATTERN

Pasta Potpourri
Party

Chapter 13

Pasta Potpourri Party

Almost everyone loves a home-cooked meal inspired by Italy's gourmet reputation. You can organize a shower based on the fact that your bride really enjoys Italian food. She doesn't have to hail from this country in the Mediterranean to savor Italian cooking. In fact, she may not be of that family heritage, but may be marrying a man of Italian descent.

This shower is also an example of what you can do for brides who stem from most any part of the world. Simply change decorations, recipes, invitations, entertainment, and hostess apparel according to the bride's family background.

Italian was selected as a theme for this book for two reasons: Italian dishes are among the most popular in ethnic food choices worldwide, and this author is a thoroughbred Italian-American who was raised on macaroni.

Decorations

Food is the basis of this theme shower, so create a culinary fiesta with pasta as decorations. Make a pasta garland, and string it above the food table. An easy way to prepare this decoration is to use uncooked wagon-wheel and small tubular macaroni.

Divide the pasta into three piles. Each pile will be painted red, green, and white—the colors of the Italian flag. On sheets of newspaper, spread out the macaroni separately. When the paint is completely dry, form the chain. Thread a needle with button thread. String the wheels and tubes alternately. Secure the string around the last wheel. Attach additional string at both ends for hanging.

For additional decorations, make small pasta ornaments. Place six painted wagon wheels on the table, each touching the other in a circular pattern. Glue them together where their sides touch. Insert a small piece of string into the top wheel and hang it. These ornaments have a lacy appearance and can also be placed flat on the food table as a decoration, without the string.

Small versions of the Italian flag, placed in various spots in the shower area, will add color and ethnic atmosphere to this theme. Look in the Yellow Pages for a flag supply shop. Stationery stores can usually order them for you if you do not have a flag shop nearby.

Visit a travel agent and ask for any available brochures about Italy and any promotional posters of the area. Hang the posters on the wall, and place the pamphlets on tables.

Accent the food table with a red-and-white checkered paper or plastic tablecloth. Place two empty bottles of a Chianti wine (the ones that are partially covered with a straw basket) on the table. Choose the ones that have rounded bottoms covered in wicker. Buy the candles that drip an artist's palette of colors when they burn, and insert them into the neck of the bottles. Light the candles about one-half hour before the food is served.

Favors

Most households possess at least one cheese grater and possibly a food processor that will shred Parmesan and Romano cheeses in a few seconds. The Italian method of serving cheese over pasta and other dishes is to shred it fresh. A large cheese grater on the table is not pleasing to the eye nor practical to operate when you have a large group. Smaller versions are available so that everyone can use an individual grater at mealtime.

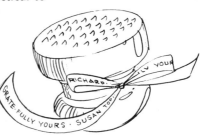

As a favor to your guests, purchase a small grater for each person. Order red ribbon with gold lettering saying: *Gratefully Yours, (names of bridal couple and the wedding date)*. Tie it around the handle, and your favor is complete.

Hostess Apparel

Modern clothing is suitable apparel. However, if possible, wear the Italian colors. Ask guests to do the same to enhance the ethnic theme.

Invitations

Card shops frequently sell blank notes with a photograph of food on the outside. If you find cards with Italian food on the cover, use them for invitations. Write the shower information on the inside of the card.

Otherwise, make your own complementary calling cards. Cut a 4" × 5" piece of white poster paper. At the bottom right corner, draw three diagonal lines ½" inch apart. With colored markers, fill in the bottom portion in green. The middle will be white, and the top, red. The card will appear to be an Italian banner. In the center of the card, write *Pioggia di Regali Per la Sposa*. That is one Italian phrase used to express a shower, party, or celebration for the bride. On the back of the card, write the pertinent shower information. Buy red or green envelopes (about 4½" × 5¾") and slip the card inside. The invitation is ready for addressing and mailing.

Entertainment

If your budget permits, hire an accordion player or violinist to play Italian music while your guests eat. Find a musician who will wander among your company as he plays his instrument. If this is too costly, simply play Italian music on the stereo to add to the shower's cultural theme.

Gift Ideas

In keeping with the theme, offer these gift suggestions to your guests:

basket of pastas
book on Italian customs
documentary video tape on Italy
garlic keeper
Italian cookbook
Italian record album
jug of olive oil
lasagna baking dish
pasta maker
reproduction of an Italian painting
tickets to an Italian opera
wine rack

Ask the guests to wrap the gifts in red, green, or white paper with bows and macaroni glued decoratively on the tops of the packages.

Menu

A pasta bar is the main item on the menu for this shower. It consists of one type of pasta and several choices of sauce. Also serve an Antipasto and Bracciolitini (a skewered meat dish). Guests will have fun sampling a little of each dish. Figure on at least one-quarter pound of macaroni per guest. Linguini is a good choice of pasta since it goes well with a myriad of sauces.

To set up the pasta bar, rent or borrow small chafing dishes to keep warm the red, pesto, and primavera sauces that follow. Place the dishes in one area of the table. Put a large bowl of linguini on the table. Keep the remainder in the pot, using this supply to replenish the bowl as the food on the table diminishes. Keep the bowl full at all times. Provide a large spoon and fork to help the guests place the pasta on their plates.

Butter, loaves of Italian bread, and Parmesan or your favorite grating cheese should be on the table.

Serve the pasta bar after the Antipasto.

At holiday feasts, or whenever my paternal grandmother invited us to dinner, she instructed us several times throughout the meal to, "mangiare, mangiare" (mahn-**jä**-ray) In English that means, "eat, eat." Do the same for your shower company by offering guests a feast and inviting them to "Please come and mangiare, mangiare."

Recipes for the Italian Shower

Mother's Real Italian Sauce

1 large onion, chopped finely
2 cloves garlic, cut in half lengthwise
2 Tbsp. olive oil
2 cans (16 oz.) whole red Italian tomatoes
4 cans (8 oz.) tomato sauce
1 tsp. chopped, dried basil leaves
1 tsp. oregano
½ tsp. sugar

In a large saucepan, sauté the onion and garlic in the oil until lightly browned. In the meantime, purée the whole tomatoes, one can at a time, in a blender or food processor. Pour puréed tomatoes into the saucepan along with the tomato sauce. Add the basil, oregano, and sugar. Cook the sauce for one hour, stirring frequently. Makes about 15 servings. Freeze ahead of time.

Perfect Pesto Sauce

1 cup chopped parsley, packed
1 Tbsp. dried basil leaves
1 tsp. salt
⅛ tsp. pepper
2 cloves garlic, crushed
½ cup olive oil
2 Tbsp. butter
2 Tbsp. boiling water
¾ cup grated Parmesan cheese
¼ cup finely chopped pine nuts (pignoli)

In a small bowl, combine all the ingredients. Makes 4 servings. Pesto will keep in the refrigerator for several days. Cover with a thin layer of oil in a closed container.

Pasta Primavera with Mushrooms

2 Tbsp. olive oil
1 large carrot, grated
1 medium zucchini, sliced
1 small onion, chopped finely
1 green pepper, cut into thin strips
1 cup fresh mushrooms, sliced
⅔ cup of milk
½ cup Parmesan cheese
1 tsp. salt
½ tsp. pepper

In a large skillet, heat the oil. Sauté the carrot, zucchini, onion, green pepper, and mushrooms until tender. Add all remaining ingredients and toss well. Makes 4–6 servings.

Antipasto

The antipasto is composed of Italian hors d'oeuvres, served before the pasta. You'll have to judge how many platters to fill, depending on the number of guests. An antipasto can contain any combination of hors d'oeuvres as indicated in this sampling of ingredients:

Anchovies   Marinated mushrooms
Artichoke hearts   Proscuiutto
Drained capers   Provolone cheese
Dried sausage   Roasted peppers
Green and black olives   Salami

Bracciolitini

10 lbs. eye round roast, cut in strips as thin as a cold cut
1 small can shortening
1 large box bread crumbs
small metal skewers

Place the meat strips on the table. Spread approximately 1 tsp. of the shortening on each strip. Sprinkle 1 tsp. of bread crumbs over the shortening. Roll each piece separately, and insert it onto a skewer. Put 8–10 rolled pieces (close together) per skewer. Then apply another teaspoon of shortening to both sides of the filled skewer, and dip both sides in the bread crumbs.

Continue until the meat is all rolled. Freeze. Defrost the night before the shower. Broil the skewers before guests arrive. Place them in a covered casserole. Warm them just before serving time. Makes 15–20 servings. You can provide each guest with one skewer each.

Bracciolitini was introduced into my family by my maternal grandmother. It is a treasured dish that the cooks in her family continue to use today.

Biscuit Tortoni Amandine

1½ cups heavy cream
½ cup sifted confectionary sugar
3 Tbsp. cognac, rum, marsala, or sherry
1 egg white, beaten stiff but not dry
¾ cup finely ground toasted almonds

Whip the heavy cream until slightly thickened. Gradually add the sugar and beat until stiff. Stir in the liquor. Fold in the beaten egg white and almonds. Spoon the mixture into paper muffin cups (cupcake size). Garnish with additional almonds or candied fruit. Freeze four to five hours, or until firm. Makes 8–10 servings.

The biscuits may be made ahead of time and frozen well in advance of the shower.

A Jewish
Bridal Shower

Chapter 14

A Jewish Bridal Shower

The Jewish wedding, whether it is an Orthodox, Conservative, or Reform ceremony, is a beautiful, holy occasion filled with ancient rites and customs. When you plan a shower for the Jewish bride, it can be of a general nature, implementing any of the themes in this book, or a shower that lightly touches on Jewish covention. If you choose the latter, the idea here is not to plan a religiously centered affair. This should not be a sacred event in the context of the Jewish ceremony. You merely want to present the flavor of Judaism with certain foods, decorations and entertainment.

Since the shower is the first of the budding bride's new life, it's an ideal time to reinforce her heritage, and also to give non-Jewish guests an insight into Judaic customs. Likewise, it is also a time to introduce some of the folklore to the non-Jewish bride who is marrying into the faith.

Decorations

Blue and white are the colors of the Israeli flag, and they are frequently carried through on prayer shawls Jewish men wear during religious services. You can decorate with these colors using rolls of crepe paper.

Another decoration idea would be to make a playful parody of the Ten Commandments. Draw and cut out your own tablets (about four inches tall), preferably on white poster paper. On each tablet (make as many as you wish), write a promising, sometimes teasing, activity you expect the bride to do for her future husband, using at least the first two words of the commandments: "Thou shalt. . .''

Place the tablets in place-card holders all around the shower area, or make a poster-paper stand by cutting a one-inch square, folding it in half and gluing one half of it to the back while the other half sits on a flat surface, supporting the paper tablet.

Here are some examples of what you might include:

Thou shalt cook a special dinner and eat by candlelight with thy husband at least once a week.

Thou shalt take a moonlit walk with thy spouse every 30 days.

Thou shalt expect flowers, but also give them to thy other half in return.

Thou shalt provide a back rub once a week for at least one year.

Thou shalt serve breakfast in bed on weekends.

Thou shalt allow thy husband to do the dishes on the evenings you do the cooking.

Think up other promises that pertain specifically to your bride. For example, if you know she dislikes attending hockey games, but her future husband referees them, make a tablet saying "Thou shalt attend all of thy husband's hockey games with a smile."

Favors

Kiddush cups or wine goblets are items used at most Jewish ceremonies. They are usually silver, gold, or brass. Depending on your budget, you can buy small goblets in these metals, or you may select imitation glasses. Since there is no rice thrown after a Jewish wedding, your favor for the Jewish shower will differ from that of a non-Jewish wedding. Fill each goblet with raisins and almonds instead of rice. Rozhinkes Mit Mandlen (raisins with almonds)  is a traditional Yiddish melody. Wrap the fruits and nuts in white netting and tie it with a navy blue ribbon that has been printed with gold lettering, spelling out the bride and groom's names and wedding date. Place the small bounty into the cup.

Another favor is an engraved ceramic plate. Order small plates, about four inches in diameter, at a bridal supply shop. Have them printed with gold lettering, touting the couple's name and wedding date. Each guest will receive one plate which they can later use for a myriad of purposes, including a ring dish by the kitchen sink.

In addition to giving one of the above favors, you might also provide non-Jewish guests with a calendar of Jewish holy days and holidays so that they'll know when to send seasonal greetings. You might add explanations of the holiday as well, such as the meaning behind Hanukkah, which recalls the rededication of the Temple of Israel under the Maccabees in 164 B.C., and Sukkat, or the Festival of Booths commemorating the flight of the Jews into the' wilderness following their freedom from Egyptian bondage.

Hostess Apparel

Jews and Christians have enjoyed the esteemed, award-winning play and movie, *Fiddler on the Roof*. One fun way to dress for this shower is to model a costume after Tevye, the poor fictitious dairyman from Anatevka, an impoverished peasant town in Tsarist Russia. Tevye wore trousers stuffed into black boots, a tattered shirt and vest, and a leather cap. You can do the same, or take a cue from Tevye's older daughters Tzeitel and Hodel. They each wore a full-skirt, a blouse, and a scarf that was tied around their heads.

Invitations

Jewish symbols lend themselves to several invitation options for the bridal shower. The six-pointed Star of David can be printed in gold on plain white notepaper. You can have the words: A *Shower for (bride's name)* done in Torah lettering on the outside. The inside of the invitation can repeat the salutation in English and then continue on with the necessary shower information, also in English.

You may also use the tablet decorations idea. Write on the tablet "Thou shalt give (bride's name) a shower, and you are invited." On the reverse side of the tablet, write out the pertinent information. Buy approriately sized envelopes.

Gift Ideas

The opening of the gifts usually begins after most of the other shower festivities. You may consider giving your bride a 10-minute rest period before she digs into the gifts. This is reminiscent of the Jewish marriage ceremony when, just before the reception, the bride and groom may slip away in seclusion for up to 15 minutes. This custom, called *yichud*, hails from ancient times when a groom would bring the bride to his tent to consummate the marriage. Today, this action provides the couple with a chance to spend their first few minutes married alone and together before meeting their guests. The idea of taking time out for a breather during the shower is a good one.

Jewish ceremonial objects for the home, and Israeli handicrafts are good gifts for the Jewish bride. Here are a few suggestions:

bagel cookbook
bagel slicer
Bible
candles
candle snuffer
challah cover
challah knife
Hanukkah Menorah
Havdala spice box
Jewish cookbook
Jewish wedding traditions book
kiddush cups
kosher and non-kosher potholders
lace tablecloth (holidays)
matzoth box
matzoth cover
Passover Seder plate
set of babushka dolls
silver cover for Bible
traveling candlesticks

In addition to these gifts, there is the Mezuzah, one of the most common religious objects present in Jewish homes. The Mezuzah is a scroll upon which is inscribed a passage from the Torah (Deuteronomy 6:4–9 and 11:13–21). This is a sacred document written by an ordained scribe. It's enclosed in a case and is hung in doorways. The Bible verses beseech the Jewish home to write on its doorposts that the Lord is loved and remembered for having saved them. You can have a Mezuzah written and blessed for the bride and buy her a case. Mezuzah cases have been made in everything from plastic to gold. Seek a rabbi's help in ordering the Mezuzah.

Another special gift idea concerns the ketubah, the Jewish marriage contract. The ketubah is read during the wedding ceremony by the rabbi and sometimes also by the nuptial couple. The ketubah is given to the bride after it is witnessed and signed. The bride often commissions an artist to write the contract in English and/or Aramaic. You can give the bride a gift certificate to have this done.

Entertainment

The huppah is a canopy which is positioned over the bride and groom at Jewish weddings. Usually made of cloth or flowers, the huppah recalls, among other ancient traditions, that the bride was led to the groom's tent for the marriage consummation. This canopy is often a grandmother's shawl or a coverlet. Propped onto four posts, the top of the huppah is positioned over the nuptial couple. You and your guests can help the bride make her own huppah.

Have everyone bring in a square of muslin that can be sewn to form the canopy. Since the huppah is five feet wide and three feet long, you need to divide the number of shower guests into the square footage the huppah comprises. Each guest will then cut her square according to size and then add her own artistic touches within the square. She may write her best wishes on the fabric using stencils, calligraphy, needlepoint, appliqués or embroidery. Messages should be to the bride and groom and may contain any number of sayings such as Mazal Tov (peace), L'Chaim (to life), or Happy Marriage. Be sure each guest signs her name to the square and brings the completed piece to the shower.

During the party, each guest can hand-sew her square to another until the huppah is completed. The bride can then back it with a solid piece of muslin. You may play some Jewish folk music in the background while your guests are sewing, including the score from Fiddler on the Roof. Remind guests that the song Sunrise, Sunset is played during some Christian weddings as the bride walks down the aisle. The chorus alludes to the huppah, singing, " . . . Is there a canopy in store for me?"

Following the wedding, the bride and groom can use the huppah as a meaningful decoration for their home.

Brides also desire flowered canopies; call on your guests to help make one. Instead of a wishing-well item, have each bring a silk flower. Choose the color and type of flower. Buy a wooden trellis and, during the shower, decorate the top with flowers. Use artificial greenery as a filler.

Aside from the huppah, you can busy your guests with a game. Here is one I designed, based on the tradition that marriages were arranged by parents with a shadchan, a matchmaker.

Matchmaker, Matchmaker Game

The object of the game is to match a guest's name with the description of the man in her life. The individual who makes the most matches correctly is the winner.

When you send out the bridal shower invitation, include a request that each guest write a few paragraphs describing the man in her life. It can be anyone from the guest's boyfriend, husband, father, friend, or even rabbi or favorite clergyman. Ask the guest to send the description to you right away. Narrow down the description to one sentence such as "He is a great basketball player who enjoys a good mystery novel and a cup of tea in front of the fireplace," or, "He is an avid skier who spends a great deal of time at Temple praying he won't break a leg on his next trip."

After summarizing all of the descriptions, type them onto a sheet of paper in numerical order. Below the descriptions, type out the names of each man with a guest's name beside it. Scramble the names. Beside each name, draw a small blank line for the number.

Pass out one game per guest; let them see what kind of matchmakers they are. Your guests will laugh at the ones they miss and be surprised by the ones they get right.

Menu

Many foods of the Old Testament are still used by Jews such as matzoths or unleavened bread. Foods cooked in oil remind some of Hanukkah, commemorating not only freedom from the Greek ruler Antiochus, but also of the miracle that followed. It was thought there was only enough oil for one night's illumination, but the oil was found to last for eight nights.

Dishes associated with Jewish Americans are mostly eastern European, the area from which they emigrated. Serve your guests an array of traditional foods. Many Jews follow religious dietary laws and do not mix meat and dairy products. The following recipes are parve (may be served with meat or dairy products). Present your guests with food buffet style. Include homemade or bakery challah bread, bagels, and a green salad with vinegar and oil dressing. You may order a cake or other dessert from a Kosher bakery.

Recipes for the Jewish Shower

Anatevka Gefilte Fish
Fish Balls:
2 cans (16½ oz.) tuna fish, drained
4 eggs
2 medium white onions, grated
1 carrot, grated
¾ cup matzoth meal
    Pinch of salt
2 Tbsp. white pepper
    horseradish

In large mixing bowl, separate and chop tuna with a fork. Add remaining ingredients except horseradish. Mix well. Form into 2-inch balls. Make sauce.

Sauce:
1½ quarts water
2 medium white onions, diced
2 carrots, sliced
¼ tsp. salt
¼ tsp. white pepper

Combine ingredients in saucepan and bring to boil. Place fish balls into the pot. Cover. Reduce heat and simmer for 15 minutes. Decrease heat to low and cook for about 1 hour. Remove. Cool and serve with horseradish. Makes 1½ dozen.

Eggplant Stew
2 medium onions, diced
2 cloves garlic, minced
4 Tbsp. vegetable oil
2 medium eggplants cut into one-inch chunks
1 large green pepper, diced
1 lb. can whole tomatoes, chopped
2 Tbsp. sugar

In a Dutch, oven sauté onion and garlic in oil. Add remaining ingredients (including liquid from the tomatoes). Simmer partially covered for one-half hour. Makes 10 servings.

Potato Latkes

2½ lbs. potatoes, peeled
2 small onions
3 eggs beaten
1 tsp. pepper
⅓ cup matzoth meal
½ cup vegetable oil

Grate potatoes and onions into a large bowl. Mix in eggs, pepper, and matzoth meal. Add more matzoth meal if mixture seems too wet. Pour oil into skillet. Heat oil (medium heat). With large spoon, place enough mixture into the pan to make three-inch pancakes. Fill the pan, flattening each mixture with spoon. Continue making latkes, cooking until they are browned on both sides. Place on paper towel to drain. Serve with yogurt or sour cream. Makes 30 three-inch pancakes.

Matzoth Balls

2 eggs
¼ cup vegetable shortening
1 cup matzoth meal
water
1 tsp. salt
1 tsp. salt
¼ tsp. ground ginger
Freshly chopped parsley

In medium bowl, beat together eggs, shortening and matzoth meal. Add about ¼ to ½ cup water and the salt, stirring to make a stiff batter. Add pepper, ginger, and parsley. Cover and chill in refrigerator for at least 2 hours. About 30 minutes before serving, wet your hands to prevent them from sticking to the dough as you form balls. Drop them into boiling salted water. Cover. Cook for 30 minutes. Drain and serve. Makes 8 balls.

Stop the Presses: Media Bride Gets Showered

Chapter 15

Stop the Presses: Media Bride Gets Showered

A journalist—or any woman working in advertising, radio, television, or magazine and book publishing—can be given the Stop the Presses shower. The ideas presented here are targeted toward a woman working for a newspaper. With slight alterations, you can adapt the theme to any other job in the media.

Decorations

There is an old riddle that can be applied to decorations for this theme. It goes like this: "What is black and white and read all over?" You guessed it, "A newspaper." Use this riddle as the basis for your color scheme.

For example, use a white tablecloth with black napkins and red paper plates. Or a red tablecloth and white and black napkins with white dishes.

Complement the table by temporarily posting newsprint wallpaper on the walls in the room where the food will be served. (Don't use newspapers, as the ink may bleed onto the wall.) There is almost always a newspaper pattern available through your nearest wallpaper store. Buy enough rolls to cover the walls. Seek help from the storekeeper in determining how much you'll need. Drape the paper with double-sided transparent tape. This decorating idea may necessitate a few changes in the room, so the hostess should be agreeable with this idea.

You may only be able to decorate one wall, perhaps the largest one, where you can simply attach the paper directly to the wall and not do any cutting around switch plates or any other fixtures, as is typical when actually hanging wallpaper.

Favors

Go to your local newspaper and ask for a favor. Most papers supply their reporters with special notebooks, marked on the outside, *Reporter's Notebook*. Ask if you can buy enough notebooks to provide one for each guest. If the newspaper doesn't have these notebooks, ask a stationery store to order them for you.

The pads are usually spiral bound at the top. Insert a printed ribbon through the spiral, one that has the names of the bride and groom and their wedding date printed on the material.

Hostess Apparel

Any style of modern clothing will be appropriate. However, if you want to create the old-fashioned image of a journalist, ask the hostesses to dress in black slacks with a white blouse and a man's red (or red and black) tie. Buy sun visors, such as those worn by tennis fans for watching a match. Make a label with the word PRESS on it and attach it to the visor.

Also ask the guests to wear clothes in the black, white, and red color scheme.

Invitations

Some card shops sell notecards marked *Here's the News*, or *Guess What's in the Headlines*. Using this type of card, you can write your invitation information on the inside of the card.

You may also use the suggested invitation described in this chapter. This invitation is meant to give the illusion of a newspaper. You can insert a black-and-white photo of the bride on the umbrella.

Type (or write) in the shower information. Start with the bride's name so that the headline will read: JANE SMITH TO HAVE BRIDAL SHOWER. Add anything special guests may need to know, such as

SHOWER NEWS

Invitation

**JANE SMITH
TO HAVE BRIDAL SHOWER**

Date _____

Time _____

Place _____

Given By _____

directions to the shower; whether there is a wishing well; if you're asking for everyone to wear clothing in red, white, and black colors; and whether you are suggesting wrapping gifts in newsprint.

After you have completely typed in all the information, you're ready to make copies of the invitation. If you are using a picture of the bride, be sure to locate a good photocopier that will do justice to the picture. Print enough for each person on the guest list, and extra, extra, for the bride's personal mementos.

Find an envelope to fit the size of the invitation and mail.

Another option is to have this invitation professionally printed. The printer can screen the photo so that it will reproduce perfectly. He can also typeset the information to resemble newspaper type. However, this is costly and may not fit into your budget.

Gift Ideas

cable TV installation
dictionary
dictionary stand
magazine subscription
newspaper subscription
new typewriter
pens and pencils
portable radio
scrapbook
still camera

Other gift ideas:
antique printer's box for knickknacks
framed advertisement from an old magazine
stationery that says *News From (bride's name)*
wooden sign for a home office that reads *Newsroom*

Ask guests to wrap gifts in newspaper with a red bow on top. Remember that the ink often comes off newsprint and may get onto your clothing. Be careful when carrying the present to the shower, and remind the bride to watch out for the ink as she unwraps the gifts.

Menu

Newspaper people are not known for preferring any particular type of food. However, they are famous for reporting on the types of food that other people enjoy, worldwide. When devising a menu for the press shower, look to your own newspaper clippings in your recipe file.

Plan a balanced menu by selecting recipes that are appropriate for a large group. When you serve the food, label each dish with the name of the newspaper from which you clipped the recipe. If you still receive the newspapers, merely cut out the paper's logo and paste it onto an index card. Glue a toothpick onto the back and stick it into the food. This small banner will identify where the recipe came from, and it will strike up conversation.

If you do not have any newspaper recipes, go to the library and borrow cookbooks written by journalists and food editors. Compile your menu from the various texts, and label the dishes for the shower by identifying the name of the book and the journalist or editor.

A Shower
Fit for a
Healthy Bride

Chapter 16

A Shower
Fit for a
Healthy Bride

Your bride may flip, somersault and do an aerobic jump when she is given this shower. Designed around her interest in staying fit and healthy, this shower may also change your guests' attitudes toward physical fitness and nutrition.

A carefully selected menu is of prime importance when planning for this theme. You need to choose foods that are low in fat, salt, and sugar. The healthy bride probably guards against meals that contain these elements. She will be most impressed by your food choices, if you serve what she might offer if she were giving a party.

Limiting the amount of fat, salt, and sugar automatically prohibits you from serving soda, salty snacks, and desserts laden with sweets. What else is left? Plenty of good things to eat. The menu and recipes for this shower are only a few of the many nutritious dishes that can provide your guests with a well-balanced afternoon luncheon.

Decorations

What do you do with old sneakers? You spray paint them a pretty color inside and outside, and you have a decoration for the healthy bride's shower! It is one of the ways to create a health club atmosphere for this shower.

Ask friends, neighbors, and relatives for their worn, ready-for-the-trash sneakers. Choose a paint color closest to the shade of the bridesmaids' dresses. Then go outdoors, or into a well-ventilated room, and spray paint the old canvas and leather (laces and all). After the sneakers are dry (at least 24 hours later), tie them together at the laces.

Hang them on the day of the shower by removing pictures from the walls and placing the tied sneakers on the same hooks. In addition to hanging the sneakers, place several pairs nonchalantly (one sneaker crossed over the other) near the pile of gifts and in other locations.

Another decoration idea involves the use of towels. Since towels are part of the exercising bride's equipment, they will make appropriate accents for the healthy bride's shower. Take a large white towel and have it airbrushed with the bride's and the groom's name and their wedding date. Hang it on the wall above the bride's gift table.

Hang smaller towels around the larger one by inserting push pins through the material.

Favors

Towels can also be used as favors. Buy inexpensive hand towels. Roll them and tie them with printed ribbon containing the names of the bride and groom and their wedding date. Place the rolled towels in baskets.

An alternate favor you can develop resembles a tote bag the bride might carry with her to aerobics class, the health club, or the gym. Look for a paper bag with handles (such as a shopping bag) that will best simulate such a carry-all. Try this idea. Go to a local stationery store and order a small paper shopping bag for each guest. The exact size you will need will be determined by what you put in them and by your budget. Explain to the shopkeeper that you would like to have the front of the bags printed with the names of the bride and groom and their wedding date. If the cost of printing exceeds your budget, select shopping bags with a surface that will allow you to clearly write the names and date on the bags yourself.

The following is a list of a few of the items you can put into the shopping bag for each guest. Select only one, or select a few, depending on your budget.

exercise cassette tape
fold-up calories chart
jump rope
packets of wheat germ and dried fruit for a healthy snack
pair of athletic socks
recent issue of a health magazine
small, calorie-counting guidebook
sweat bands

Hostess Apparel

Hostesses should wear comfortable exercise outfits. There are many pretty choices on the market. If your budget allows, the hostesses can buy matching warm-up suits that coincide with the color of the bridesmaids' dresses. If not, each hostess can wear an exercise outfit from her existing wardrobe. Whatever style the main hostess chooses will complement the theme.

On the subject of clothing, ask the bride to wear her favorite exercise outfit, and ask the guests to come in sneakers and comfortable clothes, leotard tops, or stylish sweatshirts; or have them wear the shower invitation! (See below.)

Invitations

A novel way to invite the guests to the healthy bride's shower is to send them a printed T-shirt that might be worn to the shower. Select an inexpensive cotton top and have it printed on both sides. The front of the shirt should state *Come to a Shower Fit for a Healthy Bride: (bride's name)*. On the back, print the necessary information:

Date and Time _____
Location _____
Theme _____
Dress: This shirt, leotard, sneakers, and so on _____
r.s.v.p. *(phone number)* _____

If having the T-shirt printed is beyond your budget, write the information on the shirts with special cloth markers available at many stationery stores. When you're ready to send out the invitations, each shirt can be placed into a soft, padded mailing envelope available at stores or the post office. Another alternative is to use paper instead of buying a real T-shirt. Draw the outline of a T-shirt and cut it out. Write the same invitation information as above on it, place in an envelope, and mail.

Entertainment

Assuming the bride knows she is going to be showered, ask her to be prepared to give guests a ten-minute demonstration of simple calisthenics to help them get started on an exercise program. Do not give the bride any more details. You want to keep the theme a surprise. Tell her you'll explain the unusual request at the shower.

Even though your guests will be performing light exercises, schedule the meal for at least an hour before or after the bride's program. This is the recommended time for eating prior to or following a workout.

Gift Ideas

If your bride has all of her household goods, spread the word that she could also use equipment for her athletic interests. Here are a few ideas:

exercise video
food scale
gift certificate to a health club
health cookbook
leotard and tights
new exercise mat
small weights
stopwatch

A group gift idea could be a piece of home exercise equipment such as an exercise bike or rowing machine.

Menu

As mentioned at the beginning of this shower, a well-rounded, healthy luncheon should be served. The recipes that follow are for a pita bar and dessert. Guests will be able to fill pita bread with the trimmings of their choice.

Buy whole-wheat pita pockets. There are two sizes available; buy the smaller breads to permit each person to make at least two different sandwiches.

After the pita bar, serve fresh fruit with juice or milk as a beverage. Complete the meal with nutritional, individual carrot cakes.

Recipes for the Healthy Bride's Shower

Pita Pocket Stuffings

Fresh turkey breast, sliced (no salt)
White meat chicken, sliced (skinless)
Mozzarella Cheese (It's low in cholesterol.)
Cottage Cheese (1 percent, natural)
Avocado, sliced
Fresh tomatoes, sliced
Olives, rinsed (to lower salt content)
Chickpeas
Carrots, shredded
Spinach leaves
Alfalfa sprouts
Clover sprouts
Sesame seeds
Toasted soybeans
Green pepper, sliced
Cucumbers, sliced
Onions, sliced
Plain yogurt, low-fat kind
Pita Dressing (See below.)

Place the above ingredients on a few platters. Ask the guests to fill their "pockets" with the foods of their choice. In keeping with the theme, cut several three-inch carrot sticks and place an olive on each end—like a barbell.

Pita Dressing

1 cup yogurt
2 Tbsp. lemon juice
¼ tsp. dry mustard
½ tsp. paprika
1 clove garlic, minced
  small onion, grated

Blend all of the ingredients in blender until smooth.

Individual Carrot Cakes

1½ cups unsifted flour
3 tsp. ground cinnamon
1 tsp. baking soda
¾ tsp. baking powder
1 tsp. ground nutmeg
1 cup sugar
1 cup vegetable oil
2 eggs
3 cups carrots, grated
1 cup walnuts, coarsely chopped

Preheat oven to 350 degrees. Line twenty-four 2½" muffin-pan cups with foil or paper baking cups.

In a small bowl, combine the flour, cinnamon, baking soda, baking powder, and nutmeg. Stir. Set the mixture aside.

In a large bowl, beat together the oil and the eggs. Stir in the grated carrot. Add the dry ingredients, stirring until mixed. Add the nuts. Spoon the batter into the lined muffin-pan cups, dividing the batter equally.

Bake the cakes for 20–25 minutes. This recipe may be made ahead of time and frozen.

Fruit Bowl

Fill a large bowl with fresh fruits in season. Place a larger tray underneath the bowl so that the fruits can overflow and adorn the tray as well.

Saluting
the Military Bride

Chapter 17

Saluting
the Military Bride

If you think a military shower will be all pomp and circumstance, you're half right. A bride who is a member of the United States Armed Forces is probably there because she chose to be. Therefore, she will enjoy the military hoopla you plan for her.

The military shower can also be given to the bride who is becoming the wife of a serviceman. There is a saying in the military that is expressed something like this, "If you marry into the military, you become a part of the military." A shower will be a nice way to usher the bride into her new lifestyle.

This shower was designed around the military forces in general. You can use the following suggestions and target them toward the particular branch of service where the bride or her future husband is a member.

Decorations

This shower is inherently patriotic, so adorn the shower area with bouquets of red, white, and blue carnations. Bouquets may be placed at the bride's gift area and food table.

Accent the shower with crepe paper. Buy red, white, and navy blue rolls of crepe paper. Start each roll in the center of the room where the food will be served. Twist the paper as you string it toward the corner of the room. Alternate the colors so you have a striped effect.

In the center, hang a paper bell (looks like the Liberty Bell). Bells and crepe paper are available in party supply stores.

Favors

Many of our homes are without an American flag. Guests will appreciate one, or an extra small flag on a stand, that they can put out on a table for various patriotic holidays.

Purchase a small flag with a stand for each guest. Have white ribbon printed with gold lettering, giving the bride's and groom's names and wedding date. Tie it at the base of the flag.

Set the flags all around the shower area. They will add to the decorations and complement the theme.

Military personnel are always on the go, so designing a shower favor to resemble the duffel bags they carry with them is complementary. Look for small duffel bags (key-chain size) to fit into the military bride's pocketbook. Fill the bags with rice or birdseed and place a colorful ribbon around the top. The ribbon should be printed with the bride's and groom's names and their wedding date.

Hostess Apparel

Hostesses can rent a military-style uniform from a costume shop. Do not ask to borrow a military woman's uniform, as the armed forces have strict rules against allowing a civilian to wear an enlisted person's uniform.

Another alternative is to dress in red, white, and blue and to wear a coordinating carnation.

Invitations

Let the invitation suggest the theme by using the uniform hat of the bride or her husband to be. Draw the hat on poster paper and cut it out. Color it according to the hat's true color, and use gold ink to add the branch emblem. For example, if the bride or her husband is a Marine, include the eagle and globe symbol on the hat.

On the outside of the hat, write A *Shower to Salute* (bride's name). If the hat is colored a dark shade, place a gummed label on it and write the information on the label. An alternative is to use white ink on dark colors.

On the reverse side of the hat, write the shower information, using military time. For example, if the shower is at 5:00 p.m., state 1700. Check with your local radio station or with military personnel to translate Greenwich time into military time.

The shape of the hat may not fit an envelope too easily. Be sure you can find a mailing envelope to fit it before drawing and cutting invitations for all of the guests.

Gift Ideas

When considering what to buy for the military bride, you need to know if she has impending orders to move to a new duty station. She and her husband may be setting up house in a foreign country and may not need all of the household gifts that she would normally obtain at a shower.

If you know where she is going, you'll be able to better assess her needs. If this is her first overseas duty, she might be able to use an electric converter. In some areas overseas, you need this device to operate American household appliances, such as a hair dryer.

Perhaps she will be stationed in a non-English-speaking country. A good gift would be a translating dictionary or a book about the customs of the country.

Military brides who are located in America are virtually no problem when buying gifts. Here are a few ideas:

gift certificate to the commissary or other stores on base
household items
military antiques and memorabilia
military magazines
stationery
telephone
travel totes and luggage
world globe

Menu

Almost anything you prepare will be suitable for this theme. There are many American dishes that have been passed down from the first Americans—the Indians. Popcorn is one of them. Pop plenty of kernels for snacking. Offer melted butter and salt to suit various tastes.

Hot dogs and apple pie are contemporary examples of American dishes, but there are many others. Otherwise, there are few foods that are associated with the military except those that are packaged for military surplus.

The best way to develop a menu for the military bride is to serve meals that are in keeping with the foods typically associated with the particular state or country where she will be stationed.

Look through cookbooks for some advice. Your library will have an abundant assortment of cookbooks.

Also, some cookbooks are entirely devoted to one state or country.

When selecting the menu, look for easy-to-make recipes with ingredients you know you can find in your local area. Also try to choose fare which can be cooked and frozen ahead of time.

Dessert can be a shower cake from the bakery, decorated in red, white, and blue. Or make a simple sheet cake yourself resemebling an American flag.

Recipe to Decorate American Flag Sheet Cake

 2 pints fresh strawberries (frozen if out of season)
 1 pint fresh blueberries (frozen if out of season)
   white icing (enough to cover the size cake you make)

1. Cut the strawberries in half lengthwise.
2. Ice the cake.
3. In the top left-hand corner of the cake, place most of the blueberries in a box-like pattern as the stars and blue area on the flag.

    Make the stripes by placing the strawberries face-down in rows across the cake. Alternate a row of strawberries with a row of icing.

    Using the blue icing, on one of the white rows, write the name of the wedding couple in the center of the cake.

A Shower Lesson for the Teacher

Chapter 18

A Shower Lesson for the Teacher

A teacher, or someone studying to be an educator, will appreciate this specially-designed shower as will anyone working in a school system. Do not limit the scope to teachers—remember all the people in the education field for this shower theme. There are school librarians, teacher's aides, office workers, and guidance counselors who could be given the teacher's shower. The decorations, invitations, and other theme promotions merely symbolize the education field. They do not have to refer directly to teaching.

Decorations

Create a classroom atmosphere. Place the bride's chair in front of a desk and hang a blackboard on the wall behind her. Write a message about the teacher or school administrator in white or colored chalk on the blackboard. The message could be something as simple as *Congratulations (bride's name)*, or you could list the guests. You can also plan a lesson by writing some of the trivia questions onto the blackboard. The class (guests) can answer the questions later.

Apples should be the basis of your decorating scheme for this shower. Put a large, red apple on the bride's desk, and arrange clusters of apples all around the shower area. In addition to the fresh fruit, you can buy wooden apples at stores that sell homemade crafts.

Favors

For many years, black-and-white marbled Compostion notebooks have been used in elementary to college levels. They have become as much of a symbol of education as the red apple. They're also now produced in miniature, just right to fit into a purse or a shirt pocket. These smaller notebooks will form the basis of the favor for this shower.

The books are inexpensive and may be found where school and office supplies are sold. Buy one for each guest. Order ribbon printed with the bride's and groom's names and the date of their wedding. Tie a piece of the ribbon around each book; open the book to the middle section and wrap the ribbon around to the outside where you can fasten it into a simple bow. You may also add an optional small pencil to the favor. Have it printed with the same information as the ribbon and slip it through the bow.

Be sure to tell the ribbon printer what you are planning to do with the ribbon. He will allow enough extra ribbon between the printing to fit around the notebook.

You can fill some of the pages of the notebooks with relevant doodles. Draw a heart on one page, for example, with typical school-day scribbles like, *Karen loves Kevin*, (using the names of the bride and groom).

Hostess Apparel

Teachers really never wore uniforms. However, during the flourishing days of the one-room schoolhouse, you usually found the instructor in a floor-length skirt, a white blouse with a rounded collar and a colored scarf tied in a bow at her neck. This would be a relatively easy outfit to duplicate if all of the hostesses have long skirts. If not, wear shorter skirts with a blouse and scarf.

Invitations

To complement this theme, design the invitations to resemble minia-ture blackboards. You should use black construction paper and white ink to suggest the look of chalk. Although you can write on construc-tion paper with chalk, it is not suitable for the invitation as it can rub off too easily.

Cut the paper 5½" wide by 4" high to form the bogus blackboard. Next write your shower message with the white ink. Start at the top center and write: A *Shower Lesson for (bride's name)*. On the next line, state the date and time, followed by the shower location on the third line. Leave space for any other party information. In the margins, you can write short notes to guests, such as *It's a Surprise* or *Please wrap your gifts in red and green paper*. These notes should be angled diagonally to the invitation as though an afterthought.

Check a stationery store for an envelope that will match the size and the color of the blackboard invitation. A black envelope addressed with white ink would be appropriate. So would a white envelope addressed with black ink.

Gift Ideas

Gifts for this shower can be anything from a school supply to a household item. Whatever guests choose, ask them to wrap their presents in red paper and green ribbon to suggest a red apple, just picked from the tree with the leaves still on top.

A unique wishing well for this shower would be a cardboard school bus filled with school supplies.

Use standard-sized poster paper and draw the outline of the bus as big as the paper. Make two bus façades. Draw in the windows an outline of bouncing kids and of the bus driver with his or her steering wheel. Color the bus in mustard yellow and black. Now you have two sides of the bus completed. Using plain poster paper, cut out smaller sides for the engine compartment and back of the bus. Glue or staple the sides together, and you have a box that looks like a school bus.

Here are a few belongings a teacher can always use. They will make excellent wishing-well gifts.

basket of wooden apples
blank notebooks
book bag
gummed stars
lunch box
map pointer
pencils
desktop school-year calendar
yardstick

Menu

The only food you can really say is universally eaten or associated with teachers is any kind of fare served in a cafeteria. There are hundreds of entrées that fall into this category. So the general rule in preparing food for this shower is: Anything goes.

However, it would be appropriate to prepare a menu comprised of a teacher's favorite recipes. Prepare them for the shower and label them so that guests will see you have created a complementary bill of fare.

The following recipes were given to me by a teacher. You can use these recipes plus some from teachers you know, or arrange an entirely different menu.

Recipes for the Teacher's Shower

The following meal includes chicken and rice. Add a tossed garden salad as an accompaniment.

Chicken Tarragon and Chives

½ lb. fresh mushrooms
4 Tbsp. butter
6 boned, skinned chicken breasts, split
2 tsp. seasoned salt
2 Tbsp. leaf tarragon, crumbled
1 cup dry white wine
1 cup dairy sour cream (not imitation sour cream)
½ cup chopped chives

Wash and dry the mushrooms. Cut them in half and sauté for 8 minutes in half of the butter. Remove them after cooking and set aside. Add the remaining butter to the pan. Then sprinkle the breasts with the seasoned salt and brown them thoroughly.

Return the mushrooms to the pan; sprinkle with tarragon; add the wine. Cover and simmer for 45 minutes.

Remove the chicken to a heat-proof platter and keep it warm in the oven while you stir the sour cream into the pan juices. Pour the sour cream mixture over the chicken, sprinkle with chives. Makes 6 servings.

Rice 'n' Spice Dish

    1 medium onion, chopped
    2 Tbsp. butter
1 ⅓ cup Minute Rice
1 ⅓ cup beef bouillon
    ¼ tsp. salt
    ½ cup seedless dark raisins
    ½ cup slivered almonds
    2 Tbsp. chopped parsley

Sauté onion in butter in a large skillet until tender, but not brown, about 5 minutes. Add the rice and sauté for 3 minutes. Add the boullion, salt and raisins. Bring to a boil. Remove from heat. Cover and let stand 5 minutes. Stir in the almonds and parsley; fluff with a fork. Serves 4.

Lifestyle
Showers

Chapter 19

Lifestyle Showers

Shower the Bride and Groom Together

As family roles are redefined, running a household is becoming a true joint effort. Men, who are sharing the cooking and cleaning with their career-oriented wives, are taking more of an interest in household concerns. As a result, showers are also being given to the bride and groom together.

The bridesmaids are still the ones who usually present such a party, where the groom is the guest of honor with his bride. You can present the shower in two ways: Invite only female guests (plus the groom), or only couples who are close to both the bride and groom. In the latter case, ask men to bring presents for the bride, and ask the women to bring gifts for the groom. Or, have everyone bring one gift per couple.

A brunch is an appropriate party idea for this shower.

Decorations

If the couple shares a common interest in a sport or business, plan decorations around that activity. You can also create a theme based on their honeymoon destination. Avoid decorations that are strictly feminine or masculine.

One way to decorate for this shower is to gather plenty of photos of the bride and groom as they were growing up and make a collage. Ask their friends and relatives for pictures. Be sure to write the donor's name on the back of each print so you can return the photos. Use a pencil and press very lightly so that the impression does not show through the photo on the other side.

Buy a frame that has multiple mat openings. Place pictures of the bride and groom behind every opening and set the frame on an easel. The guests will chuckle over the changes time brings. The collage will jog their memories, thus they're likely to recount many stories about the nuptial couple. Save the collage and display it at the wedding reception.

Your photography supply store can also make up a giant poster of the bridal couple. Take a favorite photo and have it enlarged to poster-size. However, you must expect some distortion of the final product due to the unusual enlargement. Faces may become slightly fuzzy, so choose only photos of the best quality for this decoration.

Favors

Shower keepsakes for this party will be determined according to the theme you employ. Remember to keep your guests in mind. If you have invited men and women, choose a favor that will appeal to both sexes.

If you decide to use the photo concept in the bride and groom shower, you can make up key-chain favors. Buy plastic key-chain photo cases at a variety store. Then have your favorite photo of the couple reduced to fit inside the key chain. Type a gummed label with the couple's names and wedding date and place it on the reverse side of the photo. You now have a useful and memorable favor for all your guests.

Hostess Apparel

Your shower outfit will be determined by the theme you choose. It is possible to plan a strictly generic shower that will not include a special wardrobe for the party planners.

Invitations

Naturally, you won't want to buy the typical shower invitations for this party. You need something that will reflect the bride and groom. A blank card with an appropriate design on the cover will do nicely. Write your message inside.

Gift Ideas

Gifts are the traditional items for the house, but look for gifts that both the bride and groom will appreciate and use. Here are a few ideas:

barbecue grill	matching towels
books	picture frames
clock	plants
dinner-for-two certificate	popcorn popper
favorite video tapes	records
full-length mirror	set of champagne glasses
magazine subscriptions	space heater
matching luggage	TV snack trays

A Honeymoon Kit is a suggestion for a wishing well. Choose a myriad of small gifts to complement the couple's post-nuptial travel plans. If they will be going by car, for example, you might obtain the following gifts:

cosmetic case
his and her scented soap
jewelry case
lodgings guidebook
pill box
pocket camera and film
road atlas
shaving kit
shoe shine kit
tissue holder for car
wallet

Menu

To complement this theme, ask the bride and groom for some of their favorite recipes. Select at least one recipe from the bride and one from the groom and prepare them at the shower.

Also Worth Noting

- The bridesmaids are usually the hostesses of this type of party. However, they may ask the groomsmen to help with the finances, especially if other men are being invited to the shower.
- Be sure to state on the invitation that this is a shower for the bride and groom, and ask guests to think of unisex gifts suitable for both to use.
- Have the bride and groom alternate opening the gifts.
- You can prepare your own trivia game, to quiz the guests on facts about the bride and groom.

A Shower for the Groom

Taking the groom out for an exciting night on the town is still a prenuptial tradition. However, with couples marrying later in life, there is another alternative to observing the groom's last night out as a single man.

A shower to present gifts to the groom often replaces the bachelor party. The groomsmen are in charge of planning and hosting this shower, which may include the bridesmaids, but most likely will be for men only.

There is no need to send written invitations to the groom's shower. A phone call to potential invitees three weeks before the event is usually enough time to notify guests.

The groom's shower will be a no-frills occasion. Decorations and favors are not a part of this shower.

The menu should be simple, and would best be catered or comprised of pizza pies, take-out Chinese food, or buckets of chicken. The party might also be held in a small restaurant catering room.

Guests should be given an idea for gifts, based on the groom's interests or occupation. The host could suggest all gifts fall into one category. For instance, if the groom is interested in cooking, he may very well be the chief cook in his marriage. If so, gifts should cater to the kitchen. Suggest specialty gourmet-type items that may be in short supply in his new kitchen.

Gardening could also be a gift theme. Think of items that will help him throughout the seasons—like a garden hose for summer, a rake for fall, a planting kit for spring, and a snow shovel for winter.

Household tools are another gift category. List items he is unlikely to buy. These are the types of tools men often think they'll only use once in a while, so figure they'll always borrow them. Included in this category are a staple gun, a carpenter's wood vice, a glass cutter, an electric sander, and a power circular saw. Gift motifs for the all-male shower can also include the groom's interests such as hunting, fishing, athletics, and scholastic pursuits.

The wishing well for this shower can be a metal counter-top cabinet. Have each guest bring supplies, such as nails, wire, nuts, and bolts, to fill the cabinet. Ask the guests to record on an index card one easy way they have found to repair something. Have the guests take turns reading the cards. This activity will spark interesting conversation and more ideas.

A Shower for the Second-Time Bride

Previously, a divorced or widowed bride was not given a bridal shower. But tradition has changed in this regard. It is not unusual for a woman to be given a prenuptial party when remarrying. This event, however, is not presented in the traditional way. You will not be doing as much decorating as a shower for the first-time bride, nor will you be sending fancy invitations, dressing in costume, or distributing favors.

Simplicity is the key here. This shower should reflect the tone of the wedding. As most second weddings are small, design the shower in the same vein.

Decorations

Flowers in vases and a table set with china and silver or decorative paper eating utensils are ample adornments.

Gift Ideas

Gifts should be inexpensive, but thoughtfully selected. The bride probably has most of what she needs for utilitarian purposes, so look to her interests, home decor, and decorative accessories for ideas.

Gift certificates to her favorite stores will give her the opportunity to buy something she really wants or needs.

Another way to shower the bride who has everything is to present her with service-oriented presents. In other words, pledge that you will do something for her such as chauffeur her to various stores for a month, or agree to do her grocery shopping for a designated period of time.

Menu

Plan a luncheon get-together. Serve food that is light instead of a complete meal, such as your favorite quiche, a pasta dish, garden salad, and fruit. Bake or buy a small sheet cake with *Best Wishes* and the bride's name on top.

Second-Time Shower Protocol

A shower for the second-time bride should never be a surprise. As a hostess, it is your responsibility to inform the bride that you want to shower her. She may try to talk you out of it, feeling that she had her shower(s) already. Explain that a shower is what you really want to do, not something you feel obligated to do.

It is proper to ask the bride what kinds of gifts she really needs, and then to tell guests.

Invite only close relatives and friends. A mailed invitation is preferred, but it does not have to be a printed card.

The Long-Distance Shower

Suppose the bride lives too far away for you to give her a shower. This is not uncommon and there is a way to give her a party via long distance. Here's how it works:

A few months before the wedding, guests come to the hostess's home with unwrapped gifts. In this way, the guests who are miles away from the bride have an opportunity to see the bride's gifts. They bring wrapping paper and wrap their gifts as part of the entertainment. While at the shower, they call the bride, and everyone speaks to her. The hostess explains that the gifts will be shipped to the bride immediately.

After receiving the shipment of gifts, the bride holds her own shower. She calls nearby family and friends to come over and watch her open the packages.

Here is a step-by-step guide on how to organize such a shower:

Prearrange with the bride that you'll call her at a certain time and day for her shower. Rent, borrow, or buy a speaker phone to attach to your telephone to permit the bride to hear and speak to all the guests at once.

As an alternative, you can have the guests bring wrapped gifts to the shower. Place them in a pile on the floor and have each guest open a package other than the one they brought. They will unwrap the present while the speakerphone is on. This way, the bride will hear all the *ooohs* and *aaahs* and other exclamations as the gifts are uncovered. The bride will try to visualize her gifts as the guests describe them. The gifts can then be boxed and sent without rewrapping.

Someone should assume the responsibility to record the name and address of each gift-giver and mail the list to the bride along with the gifts.

Remember that the telephone bill for this shower will be a major part of your budget expenses.

Restaurant Shower

After you have met with the other hostesses and have determined that you want to hold the shower in a restaurant's banquet room or catering hall, reserve a room right away.

Make a list of possible catering halls and call them to find out which ones fit your budget. Once you have narrowed down the possibilities, call the banquet managers and arrange to take a tour of the facilities.

You want to make sure the atmosphere is right for your shower. The room should not be too large so that everyone can get a view of the gifts. Check on the decorating possibilities. If you are incorporating a theme shower, you want to be certain that you can implement the decoration suggestions.

Ask the banquet manager who will be responsible for the cleanup. Find out if tips for the waitresses are included in the price. Be prepared to place at least a 15-percent deposit to reserve the room.

Tips
for All
Showers

Chapter 20

Tips
for All
Showers

Although the party themes have their own personalities, here are some basic suggestions that may be applied to all bridal showers.

- Do anything you can ahead of time, especially freeze food preparations if possible, so that you can enjoy the shower. Ask friends and neighbors if they can heat some of the food in their ovens if you do not have enough room in your own oven. This is often the situation if you are having a crowd over and several of the foods need to be baked.
- Chafing dishes will enable you to keep everything warm until serving time. You can rent or borrow them.
- Keep the shower expenses in line with your budget.
- For all theme showers, it is a nice gesture to present a small corsage to the bride as she arrives at the party.
- When considering party favors for the shower, think up ways they can be used productively. The favor can hold the rice or birdseed to be tossed over the bride and groom after the nuptial ceremony. A meaningful favor will be a remembrance as well as a useful or decorative item for the guests' homes. Favors that are practical and tasteful are less likely to be placed in a china closet, forgotten. Remember to check with the house of worship where the couple is marrying, to make sure rice or birdseed is permitted. If not, fill your favors with candy or alternate items as suggested in some of the themes.
- You'll probably want pictures to remember the shower. Arrange for one of the guests to take them for you, as you will be too busy.

Party Set Up

- As guests arrive, serve a beverage and some snacks in keeping with your main menu.
- Today, many guests will travel longer to attend a shower. When planning the menu, take into consideration the time of day, and feed your guests accordingly.
- Take time to arrange your chairs and other seating for conversation in groups so people can get to know one another and no one feels alienated.
- Delineate an area for the gifts, and put a comfortable chair for the bride alongside that space. The shower hostesses can sit around the bride and her gifts as she unwraps her packages.
- If you lack a table large enough to seat all your company, serve them with individual trays that will sit comfortably on laps. A sturdy, but inexpensive, bamboo-style tray is a possibility, or you can borrow trays from friends.

Set the trays informally before guests arrive, adorning each tray with colorful napkins, utensils, and dishes. The theme of the shower will dictate the type of utensils to be used. For example, with the Victorian theme, you would use your good silverware, linens, and fine china. By contrast, for the outdoor shower, you would set the trays with good quality paper and plastic.

- The hostess's duty is to see that her guests are comfortable. However, she has an even greater responsibility to provide a relaxed, unharried atmosphere. All those present, including the hostess, should have a good time.

The Gifts

- Arrange for someone to take the bows and ribbons from packages and create a proxy bridal bouquet. As the bride unwraps the packages, fasten the bows to a dinner-size paper plate using cellophane tape. Fill in the plate with layers of ribbon until it resembles a nosegay. After all the gifts are unwrapped, attach a cardboard cone to the bottom of the plate and decorate it with ribbon. The bride may carry this paper bouquet down the aisle during the rehearsal.
- If there are plenty of bows and ribbons remaining, make smaller bouquets for the bridesmaids to use during the rehearsal. Make these smaller bouquets with dessert-size paper plates.

- You may ask guests to write short jingles, rhymes, riddles, or posies on the outside of their packages as harbingers of what is hidden inside. For example, the jingle on the outside of a box containing an electric mixer might say, *They will beat a path to your door, once they discover what you do with this handy item.*
- In the same vein, a clever way to decorate a package is to accent it with a miniature item that hints at the contents. Almost any item from household furnishings to accessories has been miniaturized, and you can probably find the smaller version of your gift in Lilliputian terms at a hobby store. Tie the bow around it to secure it to the package.
- If you have a color scheme included as part of your shower decor, you might ask guests to wrap their gifts in the same shades of color.
- Bridal registries are computerized in some department-store chains. The branches of the main store can provide out-of-town gift-givers with access to the bride's choices of linen, china, glassware, house furnishings, her decorating style and colors. Ask the bride where she has registered, so you can tell interested guests.
- Shower gifts were originally small, useful items to help the bride set up housekeeping. Some gifts now rival wedding gifts. Showers are more pleasurable for everyone if the monetary value of each gift is kept within reason.
- You need not feel compelled to present a gift complementary to the theme chosen for the shower. If your bride has everything to set up household, consider more universal gifts. Among them are magazine subscriptions, records, books, and instructional videos on subjects that will interest the bride.

Wishing Well

Everyone wishes the bride well. This greeting, spoken many times in various forms at a bridal shower, eventually sparked the addition of the wishing well. The wishing well simply calls for bringing an extra gift (usually $3 and under) to put into the bride's wishing well. Today's wishing-well gifts were yesterday's shower gifts.

As discussed in some of the themes described in this book, the wishing well can take many forms. The traditional wishing well looks just like a real one. It is usually made out of wood or heavy cardboard, and it may be rented from a party supply store.

Guests fill the well with their wrapped good wishes. After the bride opens the main gifts, she unwraps each item in the wishing well. However, she has to try and guess who put each item in the well. (Guests do not place their names on these packages.) When the wishing well first started, it was primarily for dry and canned foods. Guests would pop in a can or two, and there would be no recognition of the individual gift.

With theme showers, extra care is given to the selection of the wishing-well gifts. If the bride does not guess who gave her a particular item, she is told after she ventures a few guesses.

Be sure to let guests know in the invitation that there is a wishing well. The idea, although it has been around for more than 20 years, is relatively new and not everyone knows what the wishing well is, so you may expect a few phone calls seeking an explanation.

The hostesses may wish to combine their gifts and buy a gift certificate for the wishing well, perhaps a paid-in-advance trip for a manicure or a facial the day before the wedding.

Wishing wells can also draw the guests together by giving them something in common to present. For example, the hostesses can give a spice cabinet as the wishing well; they can tell each guest to bring a different bottled spice to help fill it.

Entertainment Extras

Another recent development calls for guests to share their favorite recipes with the bride. Ask them in the invitation to provide a recipe at the shower. Furnish a receptacle, such as a small basket, to receive the cards.

An alternative to the recipe is a household hint. Ask guests to write a handy hint on an index card and bring it to the shower. Guests will enjoy sharing their tips. The following ideas are a few you might write on a card for your bride:

- Put leftover soap pieces in a blender. Add some water; set your blender on grate. The result is a creamy liquid soap. Pour the soap into squeeze bottles and keep one by each sink in the house.
- Do not discard an old wooden ladder. Paint it and then hang it from the ceiling on chains. Decorate the ladder with dried flowers. Hammer some nails into it, and hang baskets from the nails.

- The best way to separate an egg is to crack it and drop the whole egg in your hand. Let the white slip through your fingers into a cup. Only the yoke will remain in your hand.
- Flip your bedroom mattress at least once a month, to keep it in good shape.
- You can prolong the color of your jeans if you turn them inside out before putting them in the washer.

Invitation Checklist

- Be sure to list the hostess or hostesses by name. If the shower is given by the bridal party, it suffices to write *Shower presented by the Bridal Party.* You can then list the names individually if you desire.
- If the party is to be a surprise, be sure all your guests clearly understand that the shower is to be a surprise.
- Include travel directions to the place where the shower will be held.
- Include date, time, and year.
- Record a phone number for the r.s.v.p., and let the invitees know that you definitely want them to reply whether they are coming or not.
- Shower invitations are not professionally printed, as are wedding invitations. Calligraphy adds a nice touch, but you can also write the invitation in your own regular penmanship.
- Request the recipe card or household hint card, explaining that it will be collected and given to the bride with the others at the shower.
- If you're planning a wishing well, tell guests so in the invitation.
- If you are sent a shower invitation and it is obvious that because of distance or some other reason you cannot make it, you are not expected to send a gift. The choice is yours.
- If someone sends you an invitation and you hardly know the bride, and don't know why you were invited, or if you should send a gift, go with your feelings.

Recipes

It is a nice added touch to copy all of the recipes you used to serve guests. Bundle them with ribbon and give a set to each guest.

Gift List

In addition to the gift ideas presented in each theme, here are a few suggestions appropriate for any shower.

all-day cooker
assortment of linens
barbecue grill
bathroom scale
blender
bookends
book lamps
bridge table
cake plate
candle holders
candles
carpet sweeper
ceiling paddle fan
ceramic burner covers
chafing dish
champagne bucket
cheese board
clean-air machine
coat rack
cocktail and wine glasses
coffee grinder
coffee maker
cookbook
cooking ware set
crystal water pitcher
cutlery
cutting board
decorator switch plates
electric blanket
electric can opener
every-day dishes
family tree (researched and framed)
fire extinguisher
flatware
folding chairs
folding snack tables
folding snack trays
food processor

footstool
full-length mirror
gift certificate
hope chest
iron
kitchen bulletin board
kitchen canisters
kitchen clock
luggage
magazine rack
mailbox
mattress pad
microwave cookware
ottoman
outdoor thermometer
padded hangers
pancake griddle
patio table
peignoir
picnic basket set
plant stand
portable beater
potato keeper
punch bowl set
quilt or blanket rack
scatter rugs
serving trays
set of baking pans
set of general encyclopedias
sewing machine
shower curtain
soup tureen
space heater
spice rack
steam valet for clothes
supply of waste cans for all rooms
teapot
telephone

toaster oven
towels
umbrella stand
vacuum cleaner
water purifier

wedding keepsake book
wicker bath accessories
wine caddy
world globe

Wishing-Well Gifts

In addition to the gift ideas presented in each theme shower, here are a few suggestions suitable for any shower:

address book
all-purpose tape measure
apron
bathroom cleaning brushes
bath/shower caddy
batteries
bottle cleaner
broom
cake decorator
candles
can opener
cheese slicer
coasters
coat hooks
corn prongs
coupon caddy
deck of playing cards
dictionary
dust pan and broom
extension cord
feather duster
flashlight
flatware caddy
floor mop
flour sifter
front door welcome mat
furniture polish
gift-wrapping supplies
grapefruit knife
hand cream dispenser

hanging key caddy
ice cream scoop
ice tea spoons
indoor plant tool set
jar opener
kitchen bags
kitchen snippers
kitchen towel rack
kitchen wall caddy
laundry drying rack
lemon squeezer
light bulbs
lint brush
manicure set
measuring cups
meat thermometer
melon scooper
mini tool kit for kitchen
money management book
mountable pencil sharpener
night light
nutcrackers
pepper mill
piggy bank
pizza cutter
plate hanger
pomander
pot holders
potato peeler
recipe cards

refrigerator magnets
rolling pin
rubber gloves
rubber spatulas
scissors
shelf lining
shopping-list pad
shower curtain hooks
skewers
small mesh strainer
small picture frames
smoke detector
soap dish

sponges
tea infuser
telephone memo holder
thumb tacks
toaster cover
trivet
24-hour timer
vegetable steamer
wallpaper hanging kit
wedding cake top
wire whisk
yardstick

Bridal
Trivia Game

Chapter 21

Bridal
Trivia Game

Although the opening of the gifts is the main entertainment during a shower, some hostesses also plan a game.

Play Bridal Trivia verbally, or pass out index cards and pens and have each guest write her answers on the card. The hostess, or lady who was designated in charge of the entertainment, then reads aloud the questions and answers. The guests will be pleasantly surprised to learn some of the facts, while others will know the correct response and embellish it with another piece of interesting wedding trivia. The game should take between 20 and 30 minutes. Each correct answer is worth four points. Have a small gift on hand for the winner.

An alternate trivia game would be to make up your own questions in advance to query the guests about the lives of the bride and groom.

The following questions make up the Bridal Trivia Game. I devised this game so that your guests could have fun learning bridal traditions and etiquette. You can also add some of your own questions, even designing them to fit into the theme. For example, in the skiing shower, you could ask, "What is a mogul?"

Trivia Questions

1. Who composed the traditional theme song popularly known as
   Here Comes the Bride and played as the bride walks down the aisle?
   Answer: German composer Richard Wagner wrote, *Bridal Chorus* from his opera, *Lohengrin*, first performed in 1850. (Note: *The Wedding March*, written by Mendelssohn, is played after the ceremony, as the bride and groom walk down the aisle and exit the house of worship.)

2. The wedding band is worn on the fourth finger of the left hand. What is the belief behind this custom?

    Answer: It was believed that there is a vein in this finger which leads directly to the heart.

3. Dressing the bridal party in similar outfits originated with the Europeans. Why did they do this?

    Answer: The Europeans dressed the bride, her attendants, and the groomsmen alike, and selected people of their own age because they believed that any evil spirits lurking about would not be able to distinguish the marrying couple, and therefore could not do them any harm.

4. In the Jewish wedding ceremony, what is the name for the canopy which hangs over the bride and groom?

    Answer: A huppah.

5. When should the wedding cake and flowers be ordered?

    Answer: Three weeks to a month before the wedding.

6. During the bridal processional, when do the flower girl and ring bearer proceed down the aisle?

    Answer: After the maid of honor.

7. Where did the idea of tossing the bridal bouquet to single girls originate?

    Answer: The Victorians. Before the bride tossed it, she usually picked out a few petals as a memento and pressed them between the pages of a favorite book.

8. Who presents the ceremony officiant with his check?

    Answer: The best man.

9. When should the bride begin making name changes on important documents?

    Answer: One month before the wedding.

10. According to tradition, besides being the head of the family, why does the father of the bride accompany his daughter down the aisle?

    Answer: Years ago, the bride was sold for a "bride price." The bride's father would go to the home of her future husband, where a price would be agreed upon and the father would give his consent to the marriage.

11. A whimsical old wive's tale suggests the bride wear four things as part of her wedding attire. What are they?

    Answer: Something old, something new, something borrowed, something blue.

12. Throwing rice after the ceremony (a tradition that started in the Orient) sends what wishes to the bride and groom?

     Answer: Many years of happiness and fertility.

13. The bride and groom feed each other a piece of cake during the reception. What does this action symbolize?

     Answer: The cutting of the cake dates to ancient Rome when it symbolized the breaking of the bride's maidenhood and the future birth of children.

14. True or False: Every member of the bridal party must stand with the bride and groom in the receiving line.

     Answer: False. The receiving line may be abbreviated to include only the maid of honor and best man, and of course parents of the bride and groom.

15. True or False. Do not send wedding gift thank-you notes until after the wedding.

     Answer: False. Send thank-you notes as each gift arrives.

16. Toasting the bride and groom at the wedding reception is a long-time tradition. How did the idea of toasting begin?

     Answer: During the seventeenth century, noblemen placed a piece of toast in a cup because it added nourishment and some felt it improved the flavor of the drink. They would ask servants for a piece of toast as they raised their glass.

17. Why do some houses of worship allow only the throwing of birdseed at the bride and groom, and not rice?

     Answer: Birdseed will be eaten by the birds; however, rice remains on the grounds and is considered a nuisance to those walking in and out of the church or synagogue. Sometimes, rice is permitted only if a member of the bridal party has been designated to sweep up afterwards.

18. Who pays for the marriage license?

     Answer: The groom.

19. How is the inner envelope of the wedding invitation prepared?

     Answer: The inner envelope, which is slightly smaller than the outer envelope, is addressed to Mr. and Mrs. Jones (no first names or addresses). The envelope flap is left unsealed.

20. What is behind the rite of carrying the bride over the threshold?

     Answer: Traditionally, the custom showed the bride's family that she was leaving them only against her will.

21. Why do some newlyweds tie shoes to the back of their get-away car?

     Answer: Businessmen in Biblical times removed their shoes after closing a deal. The nuptial couple has also sealed a deal.

22. When the wedding cars leave the nuptial ceremony, they often blow their horns. Why?

     Answer: Demons were frightened away from bridal parties by the clashing of bells. Today, although we don't think demons are lurking about to pounce on the bride and groom, we blow car horns.

23. Where did the idea for the bride and groom cake-top come from?

     Answer: No one knows for sure, but one suggestion is that it came from Medieval England. Guests brought many small cakes and placed them in the center of a table. The bride and groom would stand on either side of the table and kiss over the tops of the cakes that might even be piled high.

     A traveling baker from France conceived the idea of icing all of these small cakes into one large cake, to make this kissing job easier. The tiered cake was born, and, to make it even easier, a small bride and groom ornament was placed on top.

24. What is the origin of the bridal shower?

     Answer: Having read the explanation of this at the beginning of the book, you should be able to answer this one on your own!

25. Name two bridal magazines.

     Answer: In addition to *Modern Bride* and *Bride's* magazines, there are a few other publications that guests may offer.

The
Baby Shower

Chapter 22

The
Baby Shower

The purpose of the baby shower is to welcome the new baby with an array of presents. A new child in the home, whether it is the first such bundle of joy—or the second or third or more—is an expense. Any help from friends and relatives is greatly appreciated by the parents who are looking both for moral support and to share their happiness.

Babies have been welcomed into the world as long as humans have communicated. But in the early days, the recognition of the new baby was merely a warm gesture. The concept of a showering of gifts has not been traced to one particular event as the bridal shower's presumed origin. We can guess that the baby shower evolved out of a desire to honor the new mother. The gifts industry and greeting card companies helped unify the idea along the way.

Today's baby shower may involve both parents. The emphasis of this prebirth party was usually centered on the expected little addition. But recently, with mom and dad involved in the entire birth process, there is mutual interest on the part of both parents in taking care of all of baby's needs.

With that in mind, it is now all right to shower the father. Some hostesses feel that since the baby is not just for mom but for dad, too, they want to honor the couple. With overlapping work roles, the father will also bear some of the nitty-gritty responsibilities like changing the diaper on a regular basis and getting up at night to feed the child.

These tasks are often mutually agreed upon, especially in situations where the mother intends to keep working after the baby is born. If this is the case, score one more reason for honoring dad at a baby shower. Think of gifts and party ideas that will please both parents. Keep in mind, however, that no matter how much the father is going to be involved, you still have the option of giving an all-female baby shower.

The baby shower itself is usually not as fancy a party as the bridal shower. Planning the baby shower is much easier with far fewer entanglements since there is no wedding-like party in the works also. Anyone can give a baby shower. Unlike the rules for the bridal shower, even the mother of the mother-to-be (the new baby's grandmother) can present such a party.

However, there are some guidelines to follow to insure a better party and to make things easier on the hostess.

Time and Place

The baby shower can take place at least one month before the mother's due date, or it can be held after the baby is born. Don't wait too close to the due date, as the mother may become tired and feel rather awkward physically.

If the stork arrives before the party date, hold the shower anyway. If it was to be a surpise, you may have to tell the new mother about it in order for her to comply with your secret ruse. She may be so busy with the new infant that she will turn down any offers to socialize unless she knows the party is for her and that you have gone through a great deal of trouble.

It's a good idea to hold a postnatal shower if many of the guests are from out-of-town. This will give them a chance to see the new baby and to attend the shower at the same time.

The shower should be given in the home of the hostess and may involve anything from a simple coffee klatsch to an afternoon tea or a full-scale meal.

Whom to Invite

Traditionally, only women have been invited to baby showers. But now the father of the baby is being honored along with the mother. So, if you're having a coed baby shower, you may also invite male friends and relatives of the father.

Check with the mother and let her know you are planning a shower and need some gift ideas to suggest to guests. If you want the shower to be a surprise, call her husband and ask him to discretely compile a list of the baby items already in-house and those probably needed.

Decorations

Party supply shops usually show paper storks, rattles, and baby shoes for decorations. But you can do almost any type of decoration that is feminine and frilly if the shower is only for the expectant mother. If the shower includes the father, use more masculine decorations.

You can set up the shower area somewhat like a nursery. Decorate one wall behind where the parents will sit to open gifts. Borrow a crib to hold the gifts and place it next to the parents. Make sure the mother is seated in a comfortable chair. Gather baby pictures of both parents and tack them to the wall.

The expectant mother should be given a floral corsage or a bouquet of flowers. Dad can be given a single flower.

Favors

Party souvenirs are never a must, but they can add interest to the affair. For the baby shower, you can take small, empty baby food jars and fill them with colorful jelly beans, nuts, or pasta. Tie them with a printed ribbon that boasts the mom and dad's name and the date of the shower.

Invitations

Guests may be called to the shower by telephone but a printed invitation will better insure their remembering the date. You may find many beautiful baby shower invitations at party supply stores. Be sure to select an invitation that reflects your thinking. Remember, this is your party. If you regard certain invitations as silly or "cutesy," then don't buy them. Search for an invite that pleases your tastes.

In addition to what you find in the store, you can make your own invitations. One way to summon guests is to write the informaton on a cloth diaper with felt-tip marker. Fold the diaper into an appropriately sized envelope and mail.

Another invitation is a jigsaw puzzle. Take a piece of large, white or lightly colored poster paper and draw a wiggly design on the paper similar to any puzzle. Use two posters if necessary. Cut out the pieces and mail in separate envelopes, one to a guest. Ask them to bring the piece with them to the shower where you will divide guests into teams. If you have teams, be sure to code each piece before mailing, using "A" and "B" to indicate who is on what team and to insure they can match the pieces. The team that puts the puzzle together the fastest wins a prize.

You can use the same puzzle technique with a different twist. Have a baby picture of the mother-to-be blown up to poster size. Make a wiggly design on the reverse side of the photo and cut out the pieces. Mail to guests with shower information on the blank side. During the shower, have them put the pieces together to reveal a baby picture.

Invitations can also be made from baby bibs. Buy a thin, plain terry bib and write the information on it with a fabric marker. Mail.

Entertainment

In addition to the fun with invitations, try to play different games than the ones usually associated with baby showers you have been to.

Here are a couple of ideas:

Snowflakes Game

Empty a large box of baby detergent. Refill the box with one-inch paper squares, each square bearing a letter of the alphabet. Make enough squares, repeating the alphabet until you fill the box. Give each guest one quarter of a cup of letters. Shake the letter out into the guest's hand and have her close her hand so as to hide the letters. Have guests work on a table or separate trays. When you say, "GO," each guest can look at the letters. The one who makes the most words (nonconnected and not reusing letters) wins the prize.

Candid Camera Game

Ask all guests to bring a photo of themselves as a baby. Carefully, in light pencil, give each picture a number, writing it on the reverse side. Make sure each game player has a piece of paper and a pencil.

Pass the pictures around and let the players figure out who is who. The one who makes the most matches is the winner.

Baby Shower Trivia Game

Sharpen your own skills with this game. As hostesses, start researching about 25 questions about babyhood and then ask them at the shower. The winner is the one who gets most of the answers correct.

Some of the things you might ask:

1. Who sent Hansel and Gretel into the forest?
2. What is the origin of the Teddy Bear?
3. Name one of the most famous baby cookies that is shaped like a banana.
4. How did fairytales come about?
5. How do you know if the milk for baby is warm enough?

Menu

Think of small food items for the shower such as weenies in a blanket, miniaturized vegetables, and petit fours for dessert. Traditional baby crackers can be served with your favorite dip. Really, anything goes for this shower, depending on the time of day—just be sure you have plenty of pickles and milk on hand.

Types of Baby Showers

Plan a baby shower for any expectant mother—whether it is her first baby or her fifteenth! She deserves the honor and attention. Remember when planning the shower that it is up to you, the hostess, to decide on a theme. Except for some traditional protocol, what the party entails is totally up to you. You decide what type of baby shower you wish to give. The following will encourage your creativity to conceive a personalized party.

Traditional Baby Shower

A baby shower can be a simple party with snacks and beverages. The entertainment would be the opening of the gifts. Cake and coffee would follow, and then the guests would leave. You may buy baby shower invitations and decorations at party supply stores.

Theme Baby Shower

There are several ways to revolve the party around a theme. You can address each parent's occupation and design a menu and decorations around their jobs, or you can simply evolve a theme from a nursery rhyme or a favorite children's story.

Another way to address a theme for your shower is to look at the mother's and father's situations. This may naturally dictate a theme. Or, you may ask if the mother has chosen a theme for the nursery, and cater to that idea. Here are some possible showers:

Shower for the second baby and more. Second babies don't always get the attention and presents the first baby receives, so a shower is especially appreciated. Concentrate on items that have appeared on the market since the older child was born so that you know the mother does not already have such articles.

Adopted baby shower. You can give this type of shower for an infant or a slightly older child. Knowing that the new baby is so warmly received by friends will be a gift in itself for the new family.

Lady-in-waiting or new mamma shower. This is a party for the mother of the expected package, not the baby. During this prenatal time, the woman is so busy buying things for the baby and considering her child's welfare, that she often forgets about her own well-being. It's a perfect time to honor just the mother. This shower can be given before or after the baby is born. Lavish the new mother with personal items.

Shower for the expectant father. You could have one hilarious occasion with a party for the new daddy. He is just as much a part of the blessed event and you may want to shower him with personalized presents and gifts that might help make fatherhood a little easier.

Working parents shower. Think of their busy lifestyle and hold a shower whereby guests give nothing but their services for the first few months of the new baby's life.

Older parents shower. Couples are having children later in life. No matter what their age, they certainly would feel better with your support and encouragement with a shower in their honor.

Single parent shower. For whatever reason, an expectant mother or father is often without the other parent when a baby is born. They certainly could use your support at this time. A baby shower will reinforce your love for them.

New grandmother shower. Friends of the woman whose own child is having a baby and making her a grandmother for the first time can be given a shower. Think of items that she will need for her home when she babysits for the new bundle of joy. Gag gifts are also in order here.

How to Choose a Gift for the Baby Shower

Gift-giving is never easy. It's a challenge. We enjoy taking the time to find that special gift to make our friend or relative happy. Deciding on the right baby shower gift is perhaps one of the most difficult gift decisions to make. Often (unless the mother has been tested otherwise) we do not even know the sex of the baby. Years ago this was brutal to our gift-finding search, since girls meant pink and frilly while boys meant blue and subdued.

Today, you don't have to be in such a quandry over a baby gift. Unisex concepts in clothing and decor are making the choices easier. Mothers are saying goodbye to pastels and are introducing bright colors and imaginative designs into their nurseries, and almost anything an adult wears, including designer sneakers, is also part of the newborn's wardrobe.

On the other hand, the gift-giving process is hindered by the fact that today's parents are often much older and have been out working. They have firm ideas on what they want for the baby and often have the finances to buy those things. Also, the gift-giver may be searching for a gift for a second, third, or fourth baby.

Gift Ideas

Below is a list of suggested, generic baby items. You may also consider giving your services as a gift. You can make the mother-to-be a promisory note that says you will run a certain number of errands for her for a certain period of time. It can be something as simple as agreeing to accompany her on a stroll in the park with the baby. You will bring the picnic lunch.

When selecting a gift, think about your own specialities and talents. If you're an exercise instructor, develop a routine for an approved baby work out. If you're an artist, paint a special picture in your genre for the nursery. If you are a gourmet cook, write a simple cookbook for nutritional delicious specialty baby menus.

Use your imagination when thinking up gifts. One mother, for example, had purposely saved all of her son's toys and presented them to her new daughter-in-law at the shower for her first baby.

As for purchased gifts, however, be sure you gather as much knowledge as possible about the product's safety. You want to be sure that an item is just as pleasing in appearance as it is for the baby's safety. An item with a seal of approval has many assurances that one without one does not have. The Consumer Products Safety Commission and the Juvenile Products Manufacturers Association are two organizations that commonly test products and put their stamp of approval on those that pass.

antique cradle	changing table
baby book	"Child Inside" safety decals
baby carriage	children's book club
baby food grinder	Christening outfit
baby hangers	cloth books
baby life jacket	cloth diapers
baby quilt	cotton knit shirts for baby
baby scale	crib gym
baby's diary	crib mobile
baby sitter instructions forms	diaper bag
baby swimming pool	diaper pail
bassinet	diaper stacker
bathinette	drawstring gown
bibs	easy-grip baby bottles
bicycle seat	electric bottle warmer
blanket sleeper	feeding table
blocks	floating bath thermometer
booster seat	floor mat (for high chair)
booties	front and back pack
bounce chairs	growing chart (to record height)
breast-feeding supplies	hamper
brightly colored mobile	handmade birth sampler
brush and comb set	handy-wipes
bumper pads (for cribs)	high chair
carry-all infant seat	home safety-proofing devices
car seat	juvenile photo frames

lock-on table high chair
mirror
nasal aspirator
nesting cubes (toy)
nursery intercom
nursery lamp
nursery-rhyme books
nursery-rhyme wall hanging
pacifier
photo album
picture books
plastic canisters
playpen
portable bath tub
portable crib
rattles

receiving blanket
rocking chair (child's)
rocking horse
safety gate
savings bond for college
smoke detector
  (for outside nursery door)
snap-front kimonos
step stool
stroller
stuffed animals
teethers
telephone for nursery
terry cloth dolls
toilet trainer
walker

Books for Parents

You cannot go wrong if you buy a book for the new parents. They are usually so busy at this time that they are only thinking about the infant's immediate life. You can help them plan more easily for their child's future. There are books on many topics for parents. Here is just a sampling of the topics you will find:

baby exercises
child care
childhood nutrition
choosing baby gear
developmental stages
early childhood years
entering school
family medical guide
infant and mother/father realtionships
kids and their peers
making your own baby food
parents magazines
raising children
selecting toys
toddling stage

Gift Baskets

Another gift idea is a basket motif. The idea is to decide on a gift theme and then to buy an assortment of gifts to put into one basket or other complementery container. Here are some theme basket ideas:

Basket for the bath. Include lotion, soap, towels, floating toy, sponge, face cloth, bath thermometer, bath seat, hand creme for mom, and baby shampoo. Place all items into a portable bath and wrap.

Nursery basket. Fill a small wicker basket with gift certificates to the nearest wallpaper store, paint shop, and home decorating center, and a few inexpensive decorative accessories for the nursery such as a night light and juvenile switch plate.

Time to feed basket. Buy a large straw picnic basket that can be used later for family picnics when baby is grown. Fill it with nutritional baby foods, baby cookbook, protective drinking and eating utensils, straws, moist towelettes, napkins, bibs, and soft toys. Tie the handles with a big pretty bow. There is no need to wrap the basket in paper.

Race to the hospital basket. Pack a suitcase of new items for mom to take to the hospital: robe, slippers, nursing bras, toothpaste, book, stationery, lingerie, blank birth announcements.

Mom home from the hospital basket. A box of long-stemmed chocolate roses, nonalcoholic bubbly champagne, a can of caviar spread and crackers, and any other items that will pamper her—a gift certificate for a manicure she can use whenever she needs a refreshing break, bath beads. That's for the welcome home. Add some gag gifts for the getting back to business side of being home again: an hourglass, a stopwatch, a pair of running sneakers, daily reminder stationery, a babysitter's guidebook.

Gift Extras

There are many little things you can do to add to the gift-giving spirit of the shower—and they don't cost anything.

- Ask guests to bring plenty of cents-off coupons on baby items, and place them in a small basket near the gifts.
- There are many excellent magazine articles on baby care and child philosophy. Ask guests to bring any article they think would be useful to the parents.

Before the new infant arrives, the parents carefully plan for this new human being to enter their lives and their home. However, they cannot prepare for all the unexpected problems that will arise along with the new bundle. You can help. In addition to the purchased and handmade items you bestow on the new mother at her shower, why not give her some sage advice? Write on an index card a helpful hint and attach it to your gift box.

The following are only a sampling of the many suggestions you can offer:

- To remove crayon marks from painted walls, scrub with toothpaste, then rinse and wipe.
- If you have leftover baby powder and you're being invaded by kitchen ants, sprinkle the baby powder at the point where they enter your home. Ants won't walk through the powder.
- If disposable diaper tape won't stick, is torn off, or is missing, use masking tape.
- Wear a cotton glove on the hand you use to hold the baby when you bathe him. This keeps him or her from slipping out of your wet hands.
- To heat food for the baby, use a four-unit egg poacher. Put the entrée in one cup, vegetable in another, fruit in the third, and baby bottle in the fourth.
- For the working mom: Make meals in advance, such as stewed and puréed preparations for baby and lasagna and casseroles that can be frozen until tired mom and dad are ready to eat.

Wishing Well

Just as bridal showers have that extra gift idea called a wishing well, so too, can baby showers. Set up a bassinet or toy chest as a wishing well. Have the guests bring such things as bottle caps, bottle cleaners, and disposable diapers to fill the wishing well.

Gift Wrapping

Pretty baby paper is always in order for giving gifts, but if the shower is for the mother, select something more according to her tastes and interests.

Tips to Make Gift Selection Easier

- If the parents travel frequently, and they intend to keep up the sojourns even though baby makes three, compile a list of gifts they could use to make their traveling easier. The parents might be campers and need equipment for the baby. Maybe the new mom and dad enjoy winter sports and cross-country skiing. Buy a baby sled or a special bunting for cold weather and a protective front pack to hold the baby.

  You should not have any trouble finding nontraditional, parent-oriented baby gifts. Merchandisers have responded to the desires of parents not to change their lifestyle when baby comes, but to actually include the new baby in many of their activities.

- Remember that working parents have different needs. If the child will be at a day care center most of the day, a walker or other play equipment may not be necessary. When they get home from work, the parents may want to hold the baby and play with it without other distractions.

- Consider gifts that double as household gifts. For example, instead of a changing table that is virtually no use once the baby is grown, buy a Colonial dry sink. This will be an attractive and useful piece of furniture when the diapers are gone.

- When purchasing clothing, blankets, sheets or coverlets, look for ones that are easy to launder.

- If buying toys, look for child-development and educational toys. Choose only those that have been recognized as being safe.

- If you are unfamiliar with buying baby clothing, consult a size guide or a knowledgeable clerk. Consider buying clothing that the child can grow into. You don't want to drench the new mother in infant outfits, so give her enough clothing for later as well.

- Terry cloth bibs are the easiest to clean and the most versatile if choosing a bib as a gift.

- Baby gear can be bought in department stores, large pharmacies, furniture stores and baby boutiques.

- Consider buying handcrafted items for baby and parents. They can be purchased at crafts shops and shows.

- A baby shower is a party for the mother-to-be as well as the baby. You can think about what the mother might need and give her a personal gift such as a postpregnancy workout book or video.

- If buying a car seat, select one that conforms to federal safety standards. It should be strong enough to protect the baby on all sides. Opt for one with a removable, washable liner.

Hints for Making Any Party a Success

HBL
Sat.
Dear Jane,
Thank you
for inviting me
to your shower.
I have never

Chapter 23

Hints for Making Any Party a Success

A gathering of friends or family for any party, special dinner, or afternoon luncheon always sparks new ideas, new interests, and plenty of intriguing kernels of new information. The host or hostess of any jovial mustering need never be just a servant to his guests but always must be an integral part of the socializing. Your first duty is to be with your guests. The following is a series of entertainment guides to help the party giver enjoy the occasion as well.

- Entertain in keeping with the way you live. Don't try to have a big, formal affair unless such decorum is natural to you.
- When designing the menu, choose dishes that may be prepared ahead of time. Never saddle yourself with too many last-minute dishes to prepare during the party.
- Give yourself at least an hour of free time before guests arrive. Do anything you want during this period—as long as it is relaxing.
- One day before the party, check to see that you have purchased all menu ingredients. You can throw off your organization by having to run out for one item the day of the party.
- Serve foods you're comfortable preparing. It is not advisable to try out new recipes on your unsuspecting guests.
- For smaller gatherings, check with your guests to make sure no one is allergic to any foods or if anyone has religious beliefs about certain foods.
- Always cook for more guests than you counted on. The leftovers will be put to good use after the party.
- Entertaining today is more casual than formal. A brunch is a good idea since it mixes the casual with a little elegance. This eclectic affair can be given starting any time from 9 a.m. to 1 p.m.

- Make entertaining easy by cooking at the table for a small group of guests. You can use a hibachi, a fondue pot or an electric skillet, or you can plan a meal that they can help you cook if you have a large enough kitchen.
- Invite gregarious people to your party, or at least one good conversationalist. This takes the burden of constant entertaining off of you, who will be busy timing something in the oven and making sure everyone has enough cream for their coffee.
- Don't shy away from giving a party because you fear cooking. The point of a party is to get everyone together. If you supply the idea for the party, the location, and utensils, ask guests to bring a covered dish or to help pay for catering.
- Have a buffet if you don't have enough seating. Set the food on a large table. Set trays out and have guests fill them with their choices. Then have them sit down, trays in their laps.
- If you are having a very large party and need help serving, ask a few responsible neighborhood teenagers who would be glad to make a few dollars.
- It's more comfortable to seat guests at a table. Enlarge your table by placing a giant-sized piece of plywood over it. Use sawhorses at the ends for support if necessary. *Be sure to protect your table by placing a cloth between the table top and the plywood board.*
- To add extra serving space to already crowded table tops and kitchen counters, pull out your ironing board. Cover it and use as a serving counter.
- Make your own invitations and decorations if you're so inclined, but if you don't have the time, seek help from party supply stores.
- Don't let the thought of cleaning up afterward discourage you from giving a shower. If you're having a crowd over, post-party cleanup is easier with disposable plates and cutlery. Paper party supplies for the table are abundant and very pretty nowadays. And, if you're just thinking of inviting a few close friends, remember that the party will be something the guest of honor will always treasure, so the cleanup afterward will be an extension of your gift to her instead of a burden for you.
- A picnic-style party on the floor is an alternative to any table and seating problems you might encounter. Roll out blankets and have guests bring their own picnic baskets of goodies to share.
- If you have access to a round table, use this for a sit-down dinner. Guests will all be able to talk to one another. Rent such a table if you don't own one and would like this party arrangement.

- Place cards are a good idea when seating people at tables. Guests like to know where to sit. Create imaginative ways to tell each guest of their place at the table. One idea is to write their names on inflated balloons. Tie the balloons to the chairs. This also helps remind other guests of who's who since they can see the guest's name clearly on the balloon.
- Music playing in the background is a must for almost any get-together. You might want to select a variety of styles from soft rock to jazz to classical in an effort to satisfy everyone's musical preferences.
- Don't be afraid to help guests figure out what to wear to your party. Although almost anything goes nowadays, most people don't want to feel oddly out of place despite their quest for individuality in dressing. There's no need to make suggestions for a barbecue, but some gatherings need an explanation. For example, for a special dinner, you could say something like, "This is going to be an elegant dinner, but please come casual," or, "This is going to be a formal dinner. We thought we could put to use some of the evening ware we rarely get a chance to wear anymore."

  For your own wardrobe, choose something exciting—but make sure you can move around comfortably and easily.
- When organizing the menu, plan any one type of food only once. Don't serve cheese as part of the appetizer and then have a cheesy lasagna for an entrée.
- If you don't have enough room in your refrigerator for all the beverages, place blocks or cubes of ice into the sink and set the bottles and cans in it to keep cold. This is also more accessible for you when serving.
- When preparing fruit dishes ahead of time, a coating of lemon, orange or pineapple juice will keep other cut fresh fruits from browning.
- Call anyone who doesn't respond to your invitation. If your guest list has dwindled, invite more people.
- Invitations can be imaginative. If it's a summer party for example, gather large sea shells. Write the invitation inside the shell with a marking pen, wrap in a box, and send.
- If seating guests at a table, consider one votive candle at each place-setting instead of one or two candles in the center of the table. This way everyone has the spotlight, so to speak.
- You can keep breads and muffins warm and looking attractive at the same time by putting them under glass. Your glass-domed cheese board will accomplish this nicely.

- Every table should have a centerpiece. Determine what it will be according to the party and the season. It can be something as simple as a bouquet of flowers.
- Use fresh parsley to decorate your serving dishes instead of watercress. Parsley will keep its fresh and bouyant look throughout the entire affair.
- When serving soup, consider pouring it out of a pitcher if you don't have a tureen.
- When the party is over, cleanup afterward no matter what time it is or how tired you might be. There's nothing worse than waking up in the morning to a sink full of dishes and counters piled high.

Index

Index

DISCARD